FLORENCE SABIN

FLORENCE SABIN

JANET KRONSTADT

CHELSEA HOUSE PUBLISHERS

NEW YORK · PHILADELPHIA

Chelsea House Publishers
EDITOR-IN-CHIEF Nancy Toff
EXECUTIVE EDITOR Remmel T. Nunn
MANAGING EDITOR Karyn Gullen Browne
COPY CHIEF Juliann Barbato
PICTURE EDITOR Adrian G. Allen
ART DIRECTOR Maria Epes
MANUFACTURING MANAGER Gerald Levine

American Women of Achievement
SENIOR EDITOR Richard Rennert

Staff for FLORENCE SABIN
TEXT EDITOR Ellen Scordato
COPY EDITOR Philip Koslow
DEPUTY COPY CHIEF Mark Rifkin
EDITORIAL ASSISTANT Nicole Claro
PICTURE RESEARCHER Nisa Rauschenberg
ASSISTANT ART DIRECTOR Loraine Machlin
LAYOUT Ghila Krajzman
DESIGNER Debora Smith
PRODUCTION MANAGER Joseph Romano
PRODUCTION COORDINATOR Marie Claire Cebrián
COVER ILLUSTRATOR Daniel Mark Duffy

First Printing

1 3 5 7 9 8 6 4 2

Library of Congress Cataloging-in-Publication Data

Kronstadt, Janet.
Florence Sabin, medical researcher/by Janet Kronstadt.
p. cm.—(American women of achievement)
Includes bibliographical references (p.
ISBN 1-55546-676-1
        0-7910-0450-3 (pbk.)
1. Sabin, Florence Rena, 1871–1953.   2. Immunologists—
United States—Biography. 3. Women physicians—United
States—Biography.   I. Title.   II. Series.
QR180.72.S23K76   1990
610'.92—dc20   89-71242
[B]   CIP

CONTENTS

AMERICAN WOMEN OF ACHIEVEMENT

Abigail Adams
women's rights advocate

Jane Addams
social worker

Louisa May Alcott
author

Marian Anderson
singer

Susan B. Anthony
woman suffragist

Ethel Barrymore
actress

Clara Barton
founder of the American Red Cross

Elizabeth Blackwell
physician

Nellie Bly
journalist

Margaret Bourke-White
photographer

Pearl Buck
author

Rachel Carson
biologist and author

Mary Cassatt
artist

Agnes de Mille
choreographer

Emily Dickinson
poet

Isadora Duncan
dancer

Amelia Earhart
aviator

Mary Baker Eddy
founder of the Christian Science church

Betty Friedan
feminist

Althea Gibson
tennis champion

Emma Goldman
political activist

Helen Hayes
actress

Lillian Hellman
playwright

Katharine Hepburn
actress

Karen Horney
psychoanalyst

Anne Hutchinson
religious leader

Mahalia Jackson
gospel singer

Helen Keller
humanitarian

Jeane Kirkpatrick
diplomat

Emma Lazarus
poet

Clare Boothe Luce
author and diplomat

Barbara McClintock
biologist

Margaret Mead
anthropologist

Edna St. Vincent Millay
poet

Julia Morgan
architect

Grandma Moses
painter

Louise Nevelson
sculptor

Sandra Day O'Connor
Supreme Court justice

Georgia O'Keeffe
painter

Eleanor Roosevelt
diplomat and humanitarian

Wilma Rudolph
champion athlete

Florence Sabin
medical researcher

Beverly Sills
opera singer

Gertrude Stein
author

Gloria Steinem
feminist

Harriet Beecher Stowe
author and abolitionist

Mae West
entertainer

Edith Wharton
author

Phillis Wheatley
poet

Babe Didrikson Zaharias
champion athlete

CHELSEA HOUSE PUBLISHERS

"REMEMBER THE LADIES"

MATINA S. HORNER

Remember the Ladies." That is what Abigail Adams wrote to her husband, John, then a delegate to the Continental Congress, as the Founding Fathers met in Philadelphia to form a new nation in March of 1776. "Be more generous and favorable to them than your ancestors. Do not put such unlimited power in the hands of the Husbands. If particular care and attention is not paid to the Ladies," Abigail Adams warned, "we are determined to foment a Rebellion, and will not hold ourselves bound by any Laws in which we have no voice, or Representation."

The words of Abigail Adams, one of the earliest American advocates of women's rights, were prophetic. Because when we have not "remembered the ladies," they have, by their words and deeds, reminded us so forcefully of the omission that we cannot fail to remember them. For the history of American women is as interesting and varied as the history of our nation as a whole. American women have played an integral part in founding, settling, and building our country. Some we remember as remarkable women who—against great odds—achieved distinction in the public arena: Anne Hutchinson, who in the 17th century became a charismatic religious leader; Phillis Wheatley, an 18th-century black slave who became a poet; Susan B. Anthony, whose name is synonymous with the 19th-century women's rights movement and who led the struggle to enfranchise women; and, in our own century, Amelia Earhart, the first woman to cross the Atlantic Ocean by air.

7

These extraordinary women certainly merit our admiration, but other women, "common women," many of them all but forgotten, should also be recognized for their contributions to American thought and culture. Women have been community builders; they have founded schools and formed voluntary associations to help those in need; they have assumed the major responsibility for rearing children, passing on from one generation to the next the values that keep a culture alive. These and innumerable other contributions, once ignored, are now being recognized by scholars, students, and the public. It is exciting and gratifying to realize that a part of our history that was hardly acknowledged a few generations ago is now being studied and brought to light.

In recent decades, the field of women's history has grown from obscurity to a politically controversial splinter movement to academic respectability, in many cases mainstreamed into such traditional disciplines as history, economics, and psychology. Scholars of women, both female and male, have organized research centers at such prestigious institutions as Wellesley College, Stanford University, and the University of California. Other notable centers for women's studies are the Center for the American Woman and Politics at the Eagleton Institute of Politics at Rutgers University; the Henry A. Murray Research Center for the Study of Lives, at Radcliffe College; and the Women's Research and Education Institute, the research arm of the Congressional Caucus on Women's Issues. Other scholars and public figures have established archives and libraries, such as the Schlesinger Library on the History of Women in America, at Radcliffe College, and the Sophia Smith Collection, at Smith College, to collect and preserve the written and tangible legacies of women.

From the initial donation of the Women's Rights Collection in 1943, the Schlesinger Library grew to encompass vast collections documenting the manifold accomplishments of American women. Simultaneously, the women's movement in general and the academic discipline of women's studies in particular also began with a narrow definition and gradually expanded their mandate. Early causes such as woman suffrage and social reform, abolition and organized labor were joined by newer concerns such as the history of women in business and the professions and in politics and government; the study of the family; and social issues such as health policy and education.

Women, as historian Arthur M. Schlesinger, jr., once pointed out, "have constituted the most spectacular casualty of traditional history.

They have made up at least half the human race, but you could never tell that by looking at the books historians write." The new breed of historians is remedying that omission. They have written books about immigrant women and about working-class women who struggled for survival in cities and about black women who met the challenges of life in rural areas. They are telling the stories of women who, despite the barriers of tradition and economics, became lawyers and doctors and public figures.

The women's studies movement has also led scholars to question traditional interpretations of their respective disciplines. For example, the study of war has traditionally been an exercise in military and political analysis, an examination of strategies planned and executed by men. But scholars of women's history have pointed out that wars have also been periods of tremendous change and even opportunity for women, because the very absence of men on the home front enabled them to expand their educational, economic, and professional activities and to assume leadership in their homes.

The early scholars of women's history showed a unique brand of courage in choosing to investigate new subjects and take new approaches to old ones. Often, like their subjects, they endured criticism and even ostracism by their academic colleagues. But their efforts have unquestionably been worthwhile, because with the publication of each new study and book another piece of the historical patchwork is sewn into place, revealing an increasingly comprehensive picture of the role of women in our rich and varied history.

Such books on groups of women are essential, but books that focus on the lives of individuals are equally indispensable. Biographies can be inspirational, offering their readers the example of people with vision who have looked outside themselves for their goals and have often struggled against great obstacles to achieve them. Marian Anderson, for instance, had to overcome racial bigotry in order to perfect her art and perform as a concert singer. Isadora Duncan defied the rules of classical dance to find true artistic freedom. Jane Addams had to break down society's notions of the proper role for women in order to create new social institutions, notably the settlement house. All of these women had to come to terms both with themselves and with the world in which they lived. Only then could they move ahead as pioneers in their chosen callings.

Biography can inspire not only by adulation but also by realism. It helps us to see not only the qualities in others that we hope to emulate but also, perhaps, the weaknesses that made them "human." By helping us identify with the subject on a more personal level they help us to feel that we, too, can achieve such goals. We read about Eleanor Roosevelt, for example, who occupied a unique and seemingly enviable position as the wife of the president. Yet we can sympathize with her inner dilemma: an inherently shy woman who had to force herself to live a most public life in order to use her position to benefit others. We may not be able to imagine ourselves having the immense poetic talent of Emily Dickinson, but from her story we can understand the challenges faced by a creative woman who was expected to fulfill many family responsibilities. And though few of us will ever reach the level of athletic accomplishment displayed by Wilma Rudolph or Babe Zaharias, we can still appreciate their spirit, their overwhelming will to excel.

A biography is a multifaceted lens. It is first of all a magnification, the intimate examination of one particular life. But at the same time, it is a wide-angle lens, informing us about the world in which the subject lived. We come away from reading about one life knowing more about the social, political, and economic fabric of the time. It is for this reason, perhaps, that the great New England essayist Ralph Waldo Emerson wrote, in 1841, "There is properly no history: only biography." And it is also why biography, and particularly women's biography, will continue to fascinate writers and readers alike.

FLORENCE SABIN

Florence Sabin devoted her life to science. She is shown here in her seventies, when she aided researchers at the University of Colorado by using technology that was not in existence when she started her research work at the beginning of the 20th century.

ONE

"Health to Match Our Mountains"

At eight o'clock one snowy morning in 1947, Florence Sabin pulled on a pair of heavy arctic overshoes, wrapped a woolen scarf tightly around her head, and prepared to leave the apartment she shared with her sister, Mary, at 1333 East 10th Avenue in Denver, Colorado. Even though Dr. Sabin—"the most eminent of all living women scientists," one co-worker called her— was then 76 years old, she had no need for a cane or any of the other accessories of old age. Wire-rimmed glasses could not hide her sparkling, wide-set eyes. Her cheeks were pink, her graying hair framed her face attractively, and her step was still spry.

In the building lobby, Sabin waited impatiently for her colleague, Herbert Moe, from the Colorado Department of Health, who was to drive her to the town of Sterling, almost 125 miles away. She noticed that the snow was getting heavier and wondered if Moe had encountered trouble along the way. Within five minutes, her fears proved groundless; Moe pulled up in the circular driveway in his official black sedan.

Sabin warmly greeted her associate. Moe was not nearly as cheerful. After commenting briefly on the hazardous driving conditions—the snow was now falling more thickly—he waited for Sabin to tell him the weather was fine, no problem at all, and would he please get going. When she had said exactly that, Moe smiled warily and revved up the engine. Soon, the pair was moving cautiously down the highway through the falling snow.

Despite her unprepossessing appearance and friendly manner, Sabin was traveling around the state to speak about matters of life and death. She was the chair of a state commission, popularly known as the Sabin Committee, empowered to ease the reentry of World War II veterans into local life and to prepare for Colorado's postwar future. Part of such preparations meant protecting the health of Colorado's citizens, and it was on this subject that Sabin lectured.

For the past three years, Sabin had been traveling all over the state of Colorado. She had gone out in rain, sleet, and snow to speak at high school auditoriums, churches, civic centers, and meeting halls in all of Colorado's 63 counties. Her speech-making ability inspired her listeners with enthusiasm.

To Sabin, the dangerous excursion on that snowy day was just as important as the other intrastate trips she had already made in the mid-1940s. She needed to tell her fellow Coloradans face-to-face about the horrifying health conditions in the state. For a variety of reasons, the death rate among Coloradans was twice as high as that among the residents of most other states. Sabin aimed to inform Colorado residents that there was something they could do about this alarming figure.

When Sabin became the committee chair in 1944, she did not know that conditions in Colorado were quite so bad. She had been named to the post for political reasons. Governor John Vivian had appointed her with the hope that a "token woman" would attract female voters in the upcoming gubernatorial election.

Despite the politics surrounding Sabin's appointment, there was no question she was qualified for the job. In fact, she would bring much prestige to the position, having already enjoyed brilliant careers as a professor of medicine and as a research scientist. Sabin was the first woman to become a professor at Johns Hopkins University School of Medicine, the first female member of the National Academy of Sciences, and the first woman to join the prestigious Rockefeller Institute, an elite medical research facility. Simon Flexner, the Rockefeller Institute's initial head, had been the one to call Sabin the world's most eminent living woman scientist.

One of the most well known and respected women in America, Sabin had carried out ground-breaking research on the blood and lymphatic systems (lymph is the fluid that bathes the cells of the body and helps it fight infections) and had made invaluable contributions to the fight against tuberculosis. Having recently retired from research, she had returned to her native state.

Governor Vivian reasoned that a retired 73-year-old woman, however brilliant, was unlikely to cause trouble. As one of his advisers put it, "We aren't worried about her—she's too old to be of any force."

But the governor and his advisers were wrong. Using the same thorough methods she had developed at Johns Hopkins and the Rockefeller Institute, Sabin researched the health conditions in her home state. She soon learned that Colorado was facing a crisis. Its tuberculosis rate was among the highest in the country, and the disease

As Sabin's research in lymphatics and tuberculosis brought her wide renown in the first half of the 20th century, photographs of her clad in a lab coat and surrounded by neatly ordered test tubes and slides became familiar to thousands of Americans.

Sabin, at the age of 80, giving a speech entitled "Trends in Public Health." Capping almost a decade of work in the field, the written version became her last published article.

often proved fatal because there was no known treatment at that time. Cases of bubonic plague, the disease that had killed about half the population in Europe and Asia in the 1300s, were being reported throughout the state, even though the plague was supposed to have been wiped out a century earlier.

Milk and meat products, which were sold in extraordinarily unsanitary conditions in Colorado, were also responsible for many deaths. Stores carried milk so flecked with dirt that customers refused to buy it. Vegetables were also of questionable quality because they were fertilized with the manure of diseased cattle. Restaurants across the West, in an effort to reassure their customers, displayed signs that read: No Colorado Vegetables Served Here. Things were so bad in Colorado that four deaths per day were attributed to preventable causes.

Yet any proposed health laws brought before the state legislature were immediately defeated, especially those laws affecting Colorado's large livestock herds. Vivian had been elected governor largely because he had received the support of the powerful milk-producing and cattle-rearing industries. These interest groups feared that laws regulating beef and dairy production would force their industries to comply with strict sanitary standards, thereby costing them a lot of money. Consequently, they hired lobbyists to influence legislators into protecting the industries' interests and made sure that a man such as Vivian was the chief legislator.

Aware of this entrenched oppositon, Sabin had decided to confront the people directly. If they responded and made their views known to their elected lawmakers, perhaps the state legislature would be less likely to defeat the health measures Sabin advocated.

It was in support of these measures that Sabin traveled on a wintry day to Sterling. In the thick snowfall, the windshield wipers moved only with effort. Moe remembered looking over at his companion. Sabin seemed unruffled. Even when they were stopped by a state trooper, who warned against the unsafe travel conditions, Sabin would not consider turning back.

Moe and Sabin reached Sterling at one o'clock in the afternoon—two hours late. "There she is," someone said excitedly from inside the auditorium. Moe and Sabin entered to find the crowded room astir. When the audience caught sight of Sabin, they broke into loud applause.

Removing her coat and muffler, but still wearing her boots, Sabin climbed to the dais to the sound of another burst of applause. She cleared her throat. Her legs trembled slightly, which was the only sign of nervousness she ever gave, but the wooden podium hid these movements from the audience. She said, "We think of our state as a health resort. Yet we're dying faster than people in most states."

Speaking firmly, Sabin went on to explain that in the past 5 years nearly 15,000 Coloradans had died from preventable diseases and controllable causes. "If we had applied what we already know about preventative medicine and health protection, we could have saved over 8,000 of those people," she told the crowd. The rest of her message was equally simple and to the point.

Tuberculosis had cost the nation more than $800 million during the past year. To institute preventive measures would have cost $70 million. Diseases of livestock were also costly. A cow infected with brucellosis, also known as Bang's disease, produced 2,000 fewer pounds of milk than a healthy cow. Moreover, the milk of diseased cattle made people sick. Prevention would have saved dollars as well as lives. Prevention made sense.

Sabin finished her speech an hour later to a standing ovation. As Moe put it, "She told them in wonderful words how awful things were in the state of Colorado, and everybody fell in love with her, as usual." After her talk, Sabin handed a pink leaflet to each member of the audience, stopping to chat as she went. She had mimeographed thousands of leaflets at her own expense and distributed them across the state. Entitled *Basic Health Needs of Colorado*, the leaflet also bore Sabin's slogan: Health to Match Our Mountains.

It was hard for Sabin to get away from the audience. Everyone seemed to have something to say to the likable doctor. In fact, wherever she spoke, there was at least one person in the audience who knew of her research on tuberculosis at the Rockefeller Institute and pressed her to divulge the secrets of her lab in the interest of some individual case—a friend or relative suffering from the disease.

As always, Sabin answered such queries politely. If she could be of help, she was eager to provide it. Usually, however, there was little she could do, for her investigations into tuberculosis were of a highly theoretical nature, and their applications were as yet unclear.

At last, Sabin made her way out of the auditorium and away from the crowd. She found a telephone and dialed her sister. Whenever Sabin was held over, she called Mary—who was two years Florence's senior—to let her know that the lecture had run late.

There were still some loose ends to tie up. Sabin and Moe moved into a room near the school's kitchen to discuss the presentation with a small group of Sterling's civic leaders, including the school's principal. Sabin held such sessions after each of her talks: She welcomed the chance to meet with the local leaders and solicited their feedback so she could iron out any problems before her next speech. In addition, such meetings were part of the process of making contacts and getting things done.

As the small conference got under way, someone heated hot buttered rum on the kitchen stove. Sabin took her mug gratefully, remarking that when she had worked in New York she had once asked for hot buttered rum in a restaurant on a cold day. "They didn't know what I was talking about," she explained. "I had to get up and show them how to make it."

Livestock owners in Colorado, where cattle raising plays an important role in the state's economy, initially fought the 1940s public health bills that affected their herds because they believed these pieces of legislation would reduce their profits. Sabin's speeches in support of these measures eventually gained the ranchers' support.

The group laughed at this—it was typical of Sabin to take charge of matters—and then fell to their task of dissecting the doctor's speech. Going over it point by point, they discussed the audience's response and made a few minor suggestions. For the most part, though, there was general agreement that the afternoon had been a great success. Issues of public health could be unexciting, someone noted, but no one present in the Sterling High School auditorium that day seemed to have come away with such a view. Sabin's enthusiasm and commitment had clearly touched the crowd.

As Moe drove home through the snow, Sabin said wistfully that she wished they could stop and "make a few more contacts on the way home." Moe responded by putting his foot down—firmly on the gas pedal. Many hours and several snowdrifts later, they reached Denver.

Nevertheless, before they parted company Sabin arranged for Moe to drive her the next day to a cultural center in Colorado Springs. The hardworking doctor was scheduled to give yet another talk.

Sabin as a teenager. Throughout her youth—as well as later in life—she seemed to prefer the pursuit of science to social life.

TWO

"A Good Doctor"

Florence Sabin was born on November 9, 1871, in Central City, Colorado. Because much of the American West was still a frontier at that time (Colorado was not even admitted to the Union until 1876), living conditions were often primitive. "Water was peddled from door to door," Sabin recalled of her early childhood home. "Mother stored our supply in a covered barrel in a little room between the dining room and kitchen."

Both of Sabin's parents had come to the rugged territory of Colorado seeking adventure and opportunity. Her father, George Kimball Sabin, dark haired and mustached, had arrived in Denver by stagecoach in the spring of 1860, when he was 30 years old. He had spent most of his life on his family's farm near Saxtons River, a small village in southern Vermont, and was a descendant of some of the earliest English and French settlers in the area, including William Sabin, a Huguenot (a member of the French Protestant movement during the 16th and 17th centuries) who arrived in Rehoboth, Massachusetts, from Europe in 1643.

George Sabin received a solid education while growing up on the family farm. His father had practiced medicine for a time, and his mother was also well schooled. Between them, they made sure that George and their other children enjoyed the advantages of a good education.

While helping to run the farm, George Sabin studied to become a doctor. He quit medical school after two years, however, when news of the Colorado gold rush reached Saxtons River in the late 1850s. Thrilling at the tales of the rich veins of gold discovered by lucky prospectors, he left the rolling Green Mountains of Vermont for the

In 1860, George Kimball Sabin, Florence's father, journeyed from Vermont to Colorado, where he established himself as a mining engineer.

tall, craggy Rockies without regret. An unsentimental, silent, and hard-working young man, he soon established himself in one of the many mining towns that sprang up in the Colorado territory.

In 1861, the year after George Sabin arrived in the West, the Civil War broke out between the North and the South. A young Vermonter named Serena Miner (nicknamed Rena) suddenly found herself stranded in Georgia, far from her northern home. An attractive young schoolteacher with sparkling dark eyes, Miner had left Vermont for many of the same reasons Sabin had: She sought wider opportunities than her home state provided and had a lively sense of curiosity and adventure.

Rena Miner's curiosity turned to dismay, however, when Union general William Tecumseh Sherman and his 60,000 men marched east from Atlanta to Savannah, Georgia. The Confederate armies vainly resisted Sherman's advancing troops, which left only the smoking remains of burned farms, homes, and businesses in their wake. Amid the devastated landscape, Miner's schoolteaching career came to an abrupt halt.

When Rena Miner saw a newspaper advertisement for a job as a schoolteacher in the small mining town of Black Hawk, Colorado, she applied immediately for the post. Hired sight unseen, she paid a visit to Sherman to obtain permission to leave Georgia. The general not only agreed to let Miner head west but personally escorted her through a nearby battle area.

The outbreak of the Civil War in 1861 forced Rena Miner, Florence's mother, to leave Georgia and seek her fortune elsewhere. Miner eventually chose to take a teaching job in Black Hawk, Colorado, where she met and wedded George Sabin.

The Colorado gold rush of the 1850s lured numerous young men—
including George Sabin—to the West, where the search for wealth
proved to be a hard and lonely enterprise. Florence's father often spent
weeks at a time in desolate mining camps, far from his wife and two
daughters.

Rena Miner arrived in Denver nearly five years after George Sabin had. By then, he was living in Central City, a bustling town surrounded by Black Hawk and other, smaller mining communities. Although he had not become rich, he had secured a good job as a mining engineer, which required that he often spend long stretches in the mining camp. He lived in a boarding-house and managed to save most of his salary.

In 1868, George Sabin and Rena Miner met at a dance. Handsome, prosperous, and much more confident than when he first arrived in Colorado, he succeeded in sweeping the pretty schoolteacher from his native state off her feet. He proposed to her one month later, and Miner accepted. Upon their marriage, she gave up her teaching job, and the newlyweds moved into a simple, two-story frame house with a barn behind it, on Pat Casey Boulevard in Central City.

The Sabins' first daughter, Mary, was born in 1869, and when Florence was born two years later, the children quickly developed a strong bond. As they grew older, they liked to spend their time climbing the hills that rose around the town. They learned to identify birds and made a practice of collecting flowers. (Florence's favorite was the yellow flower of the prickly pear, and yellow became her favorite color.) All told, the simple, earthy surroundings of Colorado instilled in Florence an unpretentiousness that served her especially well during her adult years.

In 1875, when Florence was four, George Sabin bought a small mining company and moved his family to Denver. Although Denver was hardly a metropolis then, it was larger than Central City and had a better school system, which pleased Rena Sabin. As a former teacher, she valued education. Unlike many of her contemporaries, she considered a good education necessary for girls as well as boys, and she wanted the best possible education for her daughters—just as she herself had enjoyed in Vermont.

In 1877, Rena Sabin gave birth to a boy, who was named Richman. Rena had a difficult time recovering from her pregnancy, however, and was forced to spend most of her day in bed. With Mary at school for most of the week, Florence, who was not slated to enter school until the following year, grew lonely. She responded by becoming fiercely attached to Richman, whom she began to refer to as "my baby."

When Richman died within the year, Florence was devastated. Matters then grew worse. On Florence's seventh birthday, her mother, who had become pregnant again, died in childbirth. Rena's newborn son, named Albert Hall Sabin (after George Sabin's younger brother), died before the end of the year. Both Mary and Florence were stunned by so much heartbreak and grew closer than ever.

Because George Sabin spent most of his time at his mines, he decided that the best thing for his daughters was to send them to Wolfe Hall, a Denver boarding school supported by the Episcopal church. Although their new schoolmates were quite friendly, Mary and Florence were as lonely as ever at Wolfe Hall. They were not allowed to return home even at Christmastime because their father could not afford to leave his mining company, which he was struggling to keep afloat.

When the school year ended, the Sabin sisters were the only students to remain at Wolfe Hall. Their father saw fit to invite them to visit him at the mines for a scant two weeks. There he tried to entertain his young daughters with a special treat: a trip down a mine shaft. But Florence, who was angry at her father for spending so much time away from her and her sister, refused to make the descent. Even when he produced a red raincoat and boots for her, which he had bought especially for the occasion, she would not go down the shaft.

Finally, a friendly miner teased Florence into entering the mine. When she went underground and looked around, she felt pity for her father because he had to spend most of his time in such a gloomy place. Florence later told him that when she grew up, she would make a home for him like the one they used to have.

Apparently, Florence's misery made an impression on George Sabin. He arranged for his daughters to live with his brother, Albert, in Lake Forest, Illinois, a Chicago suburb, and attend a private school there. Florence quickly developed a warm relationship with her uncle and his family, which provided a warm, caring, and stimulating environment for the two lonely girls. Albert Sabin was married and had an 11-year-old son, Stewart, who was the same age as Mary.

A schoolteacher who enjoyed music and the arts, Albert Sabin encouraged his nieces to read the books on his library shelf and enabled Florence to take piano lessons. He was also a nature lover, and he often took the children on long walks, pointing out interesting plants and animals. Amid this nurturing atmosphere, Florence blossomed.

In 1881, Albert Sabin took his nieces to Saxtons River to visit their paternal grandparents. At first, the girls thought that the elderly Sabins were far too imposing. Their grandmother, for instance, would not allow the girls to have cookies or milk until they had done their chores, and she warned Florence not to become vain over her curly hair. Nevertheless, their grandparents proved to be quite loving, and the girls began to enjoy their stay in Vermont.

Florence's grandmother took special pleasure in discussing the Sabin family tree. The family patriarch was William Sabin (named after the first Sabin to reach America's shores), who sired 20 children. One of his sons, Levi Sabin, graduated from medical school in 1798 and became the first doctor in the family. "Too bad you're not a boy," Florence was reportedly told by her grandmother, "you would have made a good doctor." Outraged by this remark,

An 1865 photograph of 15th Street in Denver, which was still a rough-and-tumble frontier outpost when the Sabins moved there 10 years later.

In 1878, Florence and Mary Sabin—at the ages of 7 and 9,
respectively—were sent to the Denver boarding school known as
Wolfe Hall. The school is shown here around the time they attended
the institution.

Florence vowed to become a doctor anyway.

In the fall of 1883, when she was 12, Florence returned to Vermont and attended the Vermont Academy, which was located in Saxtons River. A private school with a solid reputation, the academy attracted students from all over the United States. But that January at midterm her grandmother died, and Florence was sent back to Chicago, grief stricken at the loss of yet another maternal figure.

In 1885, both Mary and Florence returned to the Vermont Academy as boarding students. Intelligent and diligent, the girls did well at the demanding school. In her spare time, Florence devoted herself to her piano playing. She played so often, in fact, that Albert Sabin was persuaded to buy her a piano to keep at school.

In 1887, Mary graduated from the Vermont Academy and entered Smith College in Northampton, Massachusetts. Florence journeyed to Chicago to spend the winter with her uncle and study piano. When she returned to the academy, she brought along some piano exercises. After a while, another student became so annoyed at hearing the drills repeated so often that she asked Sabin to please play something fun instead. Sabin replied that she was not playing for fun—she was studying to become a concert pianist. Upon hearing that, the girl told Florence that she was just an ordinary player and would never realize her dream.

But Florence was not one to be stifled by criticism. She knew that the girl's

Albert Sabin, Jr., was among the cousins with whom Florence lived and played in her uncle's home in Lake Forest, Illinois.

Sabin's paternal grandmother liked to tell Florence about the long-established Sabin clan in Vermont, including (left to right) Henry Wells Sabin, William Cullen Sabin, and Elisha Stearns Sabin, sons of Levi Sabin, who in 1798 became the first Sabin to earn a medical degree.

remark was true, already suspecting that becoming a great musician was beyond her ability. As a result, her schoolmate's remark accelerated a significant switch in interests.

For what Florence loved most, after music, was science class. The progressive Vermont Academy offered laboratory courses that allowed the students to perform original research, and she plunged into them with her usual intensity. Florence soon resolved to be the best science student at school: If she could not excel at piano, she would excel in science.

In the laboratory, Florence Sabin experienced none of the discouragement she often felt when studying piano. From the start, she was a gifted science student. Before long, her natural shyness and the air of isolation that often surrounded her receded, and she emerged as a popular as well as a successful student. She was elected class president in her senior year. Only the death of her grandfather a month before graduation marred Sabin's last term at the academy. She hid her distress and graduated with honors.

In 1888, Sabin enrolled in Smith College. Established just 13 years before Sabin enrolled, Smith was the first women's school in the country to grant an advanced academic degree and was an exciting place for a woman to study. Feminist ideas flowed freely on campus. In the late 1800s, when higher education for women, who were barred from the prestigious all-male eastern universities and colleges, was a rela-

Florence's uncle, Albert Sabin, was an extremely conscientious and caring man. When Florence was in boarding school in Vermont, he corresponded with her regularly and even bought her a piano.

tively new concept, Smith's founders were determined to give women an education equal in quality to that provided in the best men's schools.

Florence Sabin lived with her sister, who was a junior at Smith. They shared a room in a Northampton boardinghouse. Dr. Grace Preston, the school physician and a pioneer in gaining recognition for female doctors, lived in the same boardinghouse. Noting Florence's interest in science, Preston became her friend and adviser.

Sabin's hard work and natural talent were soon noticed by others as well. As a freshman, she was invited to join the exclusive Colloquium, a group of 25 honor students who met individually with one of the school's popular science professors. Sabin was also invited to attend "chemical tea parties"; enthusiastic science students held afternoon teas in one of the science labs, where they stirred tea with test tubes and drank from glass beakers.

Preston encouraged Sabin in her studies. The doctor told her about interesting developments in Baltimore, Maryland, such as a new university, called the Johns Hopkins, that was being established. The school was to operate under the most advanced ideas in medical education, and—most exciting to female physicians such as Preston— it was to include a medical school that would admit women on an equal basis with men, a revolutionary idea at that time. Noting Sabin's high grades and excellent work in the laboratory, Preston encouraged Sabin to apply.

Sabin eagerly questioned Preston about the cost. The doctor advised Sabin not to worry about finances. Just get enough money together for the first year, Preston suggested. The rest would take care of itself. Sabin decided to heed Preston's advice.

When Sabin returned to Denver after her junior year, she told her father and sister of her plans to study medicine. Mary Sabin, who was now teaching mathematics at their old boarding school, Wolfe Hall, took Florence aside to explain that their father's mining company was in financial straits and that she should not tax him by requesting more money for school. Florence did not raise the topic again, nor did she mention finances to her father. But her sister's talk did nothing to end her resolve to attend medical school.

Sabin went back to Smith, determined to earn the money she needed on her own. During her senior year, she tutored other students and began to save a small amount. In 1893, the same year that Johns Hopkins Medical School finally opened, she graduated with honors from Smith. But she still did not have enough money to attend medical school, so she returned to Denver intent on saving money. Like Mary, she took a job at Wolfe Hall, where she taught history, zoology, and algebra. The sisters lived cheaply in their father's boardinghouse, and Florence was able to save most of her salary during the two years she spent there.

At Wolfe Hall, Sabin initiated "nature walks" during which she pointed

Florence's sister, Mary, around the time she graduated from Smith College in 1891. Shortly thereafter, she returned to Colorado to teach at Wolfe Hall.

Sabin graduated from Smith College two years after her sister, Mary, did. Although Florence hoped to begin medical school immediately, financial constraints forced her to delay her entrance until 1896.

out plants, birds, and wildlife to her students as they strolled through wooded glades and ended their outing with a picnic. The parents of one delighted child brought Sabin's walks to the attention of a rich Denver matron, Ella Strong Denison, who persuaded Florence and Mary to come to the Denison family's summer retreat in Wisconsin. There, they taught a group of eight youngsters—Denison's children, nieces, and nephews—about nature. One of the children, Ned Sheldon, later became a well-known dramatist and a good friend of Sabin's.

In the fall of 1895, Sabin was offered—and accepted—a teaching position at Smith College: She was to substitute for a zoology professor during the instructor's yearlong leave of absence. In the summer of 1896, Sabin received another significant honor: She was awarded a fellowship to work as an assistant at the Marine Biological Laboratories in Woods Hole, Massachusetts. These labs, located in the village of Woods Hole, on the southwest tip of Cape Cod, have long been a training ground for eminent biologists.

Sabin worked hard at Woods Hole, assisting a number of scientists in their lab work, perfecting her skills with the microscope, and taking long walks by the ocean to clear her head at the end of a busy workday. The 24 year old also managed to save a fair amount of money from the fellowship. By the time the summer was over, she had saved enough money to enter medical school.

Sabin was still a young woman when she published her surprising discoveries about the lymphatic system in 1903, at the end of her medical training.

THREE

"Hen Medic"

When Florence Sabin arrived in Baltimore in October 1896, she found a crowded, aging city featuring narrow back streets, a maze of even narrower alleyways, and a series of row houses with dirty marble steps. The new Johns Hopkins University was beginning to build its campus, to be called Homewood, in the beautiful northern end of the city, but three years after it opened, the school's redbrick buildings were still crammed among the ramshackle architecture of downtown Baltimore. The hospital and medical school were located in the least desirable area of all—East Baltimore—and they consisted of dingy, low buildings with a view of the railroad tracks.

Although some complained about these ugly surroundings, Sabin did not. Thrilled to be in Baltimore after her long years of saving and preparation, she settled herself—with some excitement—into the dormitory reserved for women. Male students derisively referred to these lodgings as the Hen House.

The Hopkins, as the new medical school came to be called, had a colorful history. In the late 1800s, the institutions in the United States that offered a medical education were not especially demanding. In fact, these schools had no real admission requirements: The ability to read and write was often considered enough preparation. Moreover, the medical schools were in no way standardized, and all were undergraduate institutions. Anyone seriously interested in studying medicine had to go to Europe, where standards were much higher and the training was much more rigorous. German universities, with their advanced laboratory methods and highly educated staffs, were considered the best places to study medicine.

The founders of the Hopkins intended their medical school to be the finest in America and a true rival to

When Sabin enrolled at Johns Hopkins Medical School in 1896, three years after it first opened, the institution's Baltimore campus had not yet been completed. Nevertheless, the ramshackle surroundings could not dim Sabin's enthusiasm for her new school.

those in Europe. But before the institution opened its doors for the first time, the school's president, Daniel Coit Gilman, found that the school lacked enough funds to hold classes. The school's unsettled admissions policy added to a delay in the opening. Some founders felt that a college degree and a background in chemistry and physics should be required of applicants; others felt these requirements were too exacting.

In 1890, four women—daughters of Johns Hopkins trustees—founded the Women's Fund Committee and became involved in efforts to raise money for the proposed school. These women believed that high standards for admission should be maintained, and they also felt that women should be admitted to the school on the same basis as men. One of the women, M. Carey Thomas, had been denied admission to a Ph.D. program owing to her gender and had been compelled to get her degree in Europe; a crusader for the cause of quality higher education for women, she later became president of Bryn Mawr College. Another committee member was Mary Elizabeth Garrett, heiress to the wealthy owner of the Baltimore & Ohio Railroad. Urged on by her friend Thomas, Garrett contributed the bulk of the $500,000 needed by Gilman to open the medical school.

Gilman was reluctant to take their bequest, however, when he learned of the women's views. He felt their proposed standards were too high. More to the point, he did not believe that women belonged in medical school. Eventually, Gilman acceded to the women's demands because he needed their money. Before he did so, however, he insisted on a change in wording in the statement of the school's aims and standards. Rather than admitting women on the "the same basis as men," the Hopkins would admit them on "an equal basis with men." Gilman thought the new wording reflected that women were not the same as men and did not have the same intellectual capacities; in his words, it would prevent female students from "becoming discouraged."

Although the change displeased the Women's Fund Committee, they decided not to argue with Gilman. When the Hopkins first opened its doors in 1893, 3 of the 22 members of its initial class were women. From that time on, the Women of Baltimore, as the Hopkins benefactors were sometimes called, kept an interested eye on the female medical students.

Martha Carey Thomas was instrumental in upgrading the admission standards of Johns Hopkins Medical School and allowing the entrance of women to the program. She later became a professor of English, dean, and president of Bryn Mawr College in Pennsylvania.

Daniel Coit Gilman, president of Johns Hopkins Medical School at the turn of the century, did not think women possessed the same scientific ability as did men. Only the funds raised by the Women of Baltimore, a small group of benefactors, persuaded him to permit women to enroll "on an equal basis" at Johns Hopkins.

Prominent among these students in 1896 was Florence Sabin. Her academic record was better than that of most of the men in her freshman class, and her teaching experience at Smith and tenure at Woods Hole gave her a further edge. The Women of Baltimore expected a great deal from her.

Sabin, awed and elated to find herself in medical school, moved eagerly through her first-year courses in anatomy, biochemistry, physiology, pharmacology, and bacteriology. In this last class, which involved the study of microorganisms, she encountered the concept of stains—dyes used to color parts of a specimen so it could be observed more clearly under a microscope—and was fascinated by the process. Almost immediately, she became an expert at the delicate procedures that staining involved.

One day, leaning over a laboratory table to peer into her microscope, Sabin felt that someone was looking over her shoulder. She turned around and saw a slim, quiet young man. To the serious, bespectacled Sabin, he appeared to be another medical student.

When the man asked to see the slide Sabin was working on, she got up so he could look into her microscope. "Nice," he said. Then he moved to the next student.

This was Florence Sabin's introduction to the man who was to become her mentor for the next 20 years: Franklin Paine Mall. A brilliant anatomist who had studied in Germany at the University of Leipzig with the best medical minds of his day, Mall was noted for his understated approach to students, whom he never praised. They knew of his regard for them only through the degree of interest he expressed in their work.

Mall did not believe in lectures or texts. He thought that anatomy (the study of the structure of organisms, especially the human body) should be taught chiefly in the laboratory. A sign in his laboratory suggested as much; it read: Your Body Is Your Textbook.

With great difficulty, because Maryland had strict laws regarding the disposition of corpses, Pall arranged for a steady supply of cadavers so his students could teach themselves anatomy by means of dissecting dead bodies. Sabin later explained, "Bodies were hard to obtain. . . . The prevailing method for embalming—namely injecting with arsenic—did not make them suitable for slow and painstaking dissection by untrained students. . . . The work was carried on only when the weather was sufficiently cold."

The dignified, world-renowned Mall was only 34 years old when Sabin first met him. As she later said in her biography of him, published in 1934, "Mall looked mild, even unimpressive, and one might easily pass him by. But he was a man of power who loved to fight for ideals, and by sheer force of his willpower he made people go his way."

Among Mall's unorthodox ideas was that only the most talented students— perhaps "one in every 10,000"—should be trained as "investigators," or research scientists. As the distinguished, often rather dour man began to stop by

Sabin's microscope or dissecting table more and more often, it became apparent to the entire class that he had singled out Sabin as one of those talented students. She thrilled at the thought and grew determined to live up to Mall's exacting standards.

Toward the end of Sabin's sophomore year, Mall assigned her to a research project on lymphatics, the system of fluids that bathe each cell of the body and cleanse the blood. The lymphatic system—which is essential to the body's defense against diseases—was not well understood at that time (even today, many mysteries still surround it). When Sabin started her project, it was believed that the lymphatic system, which is a vessel system like the blood system, grew independently of the blood vessels and connected with them through open endings.

After injecting the lymph vessels of pig embryos with colored dyes and examining them carefully under her microscope, Sabin began to suspect that rather than being an independent system, the lymphatic system budded out from existing blood vessels and continued outward in channels by a process of further budding. Most striking of all, Sabin was certain that the ends of the lymphatic channels were not open but closed. She carefully assembled her painstakingly prepared slides and wrote up meticulous notes of her observations. Then she took her conclusions to Mall.

Sabin had taken her research much further than Mall expected. He was fascinated by her results—but not yet convinced by them, although he could find nothing wrong. The people with whom Mall had studied all believed that the lymphatic endings were open. He told Sabin to repeat her experiments to further support her findings.

Impressed by Sabin in spite of his skepticism, Mall encouraged her to publish her first academic paper, which was on the nervous system. She had written the paper shortly after her arrival at the Hopkins. When the paper was accepted by a prominent medical journal, an overjoyed Sabin promptly sent a copy to her father in Colorado. Sadly, she never knew his response. George Sabin had died suddenly that December.

In response to her father's death, Sabin, whose shyness had abated in the glow of attention from Mall, became somewhat withdrawn. Albert Sabin, who had also received a copy of his niece's paper, continued to encourage her, telling Florence that whatever the controversy over her lymphatics research, "your old Uncle will love you still and believe you are the best of the pack." Accordingly, Sabin began to cheer up as she entered her junior year.

In the fall of 1897, Sabin began to study with Dr. William Osler, who convened his classes in the typhoid wards of Baltimore. His medical students learned while helping to treat desperately ill patients. In classes such as these, Sabin began to acquire a reputation as unflappable and down-to-earth, especially when faced with supposedly sensitive issues pertaining to the training of "hen medics," as

women doctors were insultingly called. In the 19th century, popular opinion held that proper young women should be outraged or embarrassed by references to the realities of the human body. Sabin and most of her female colleagues could not help but find this view ridiculous. Yet male students persisted in teasing them about their "improper" roles.

A group of male students went so far as to send sweet pea corsages to some of the school's female students prior to a lecture on diabetes. Upset that their joke evoked no response—"sweet pea" being a reference to the high glucose (sugar) level in the urine of diabetic patients—the male students watched in annoyance as the female students pinned the corsages to their dresses. "Don't you get it?" one of the men demanded.

"Of course we do," Sabin replied. "But why waste them? We don't get corsages often."

The young man remarked indignantly that "nothing phases Flossie." And indeed, that summed up Sabin's reputation in medical school. The references to "sex differences" and anatomical details that sometimes upset other female students rolled right off Sabin's back.

"Women get everything they deserve in this world, and needn't think they are discriminated against," Sabin maintained. "They can have whatever they are willing to work for." She did not feel held back by her sex and never tried to take advantage of it. She truly believed men and women had equal

Franklin Paine Mall, a respected anatomist, singled out Sabin as an especially talented student and guided her early research. His methods and example inspired her throughout her long career.

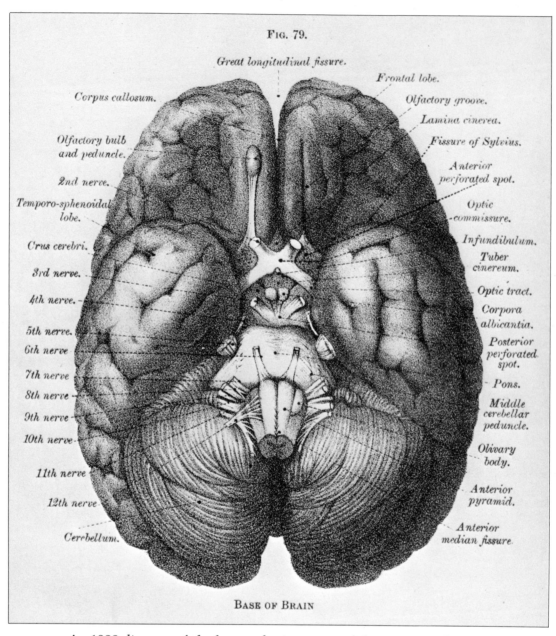

FIG. 79.

Great longitudinal fissure.

Frontal lobe.

Corpus callosum.

Olfactory groove.

Lamina cinerea.

Olfactory bulb
and peduncle.

Fissure of Sylvius.

2nd nerve.

Anterior
perforated spot.

Temporo-sphenoidal
lobe.

Optic
commissure.

Crus cerebri.

Infundibulum.

3rd nerve.

Tuber
cinereum.

4th nerve.

Optic tract.

Corpora
albicantia.

5th nerve.

Posterior
perforated
spot.

6th nerve

7th nerve

Pons.

8th nerve

Middle
cerebellar
peduncle.

9th nerve

10th nerve

Olivary
body.

11th nerve

Anterior
pyramid.

12th nerve

Anterior
median fissure.

Cerebellum.

BASE OF BRAIN

*An 1899 diagram of the human brain, a part of the anatomy that
served as an early topic of study for Sabin. Her first book,* An Atlas
of the Medulla and Midbrain, *was published two years later and
contributed greatly to her contemporaries' understanding of the
brain's structure.*

capacities and chose to prove herself through hard work.

During her senior year, Sabin began, at Mall's suggestion, a series of notes and drawings on the brain of a newborn infant. In compiling the information, Sabin made use of some new slides that Mall had lent to her and published her research in 1901 as *An Atlas of the Medulla and Midbrain*. The book was, quite literally, an atlas: a verbal, pictorial, and very complete map of the brain as it was understood at the turn of the century. Narrated in the first person and written in tight, clear prose, the book takes the reader on a journey from the medulla (the beginning of the spinal cord at the base of the brain) to the midbrain, then to the "olives" (two oval-shaped bodies on either side of the medulla), and finally through the various nerve systems.

Sabin's editors said of *An Atlas of the Medulla and Midbrain*, "We believe, and a number of well-known teachers in several large universities have agreed in this opinion, that this little Atlas will offer a valuable new remedy." Others quickly agreed. The atlas became the definitive work on the topic and remained so for at least 30 years. Today, it is still found in medical school libraries.

Sabin's final project as a senior was the usual prerequisite for graduation: to deliver nine babies. Sabin carefully managed the feat, although delivering the babies gave her, she said, a "case of nerves." She vastly preferred the quiet of the research lab to daily practice.

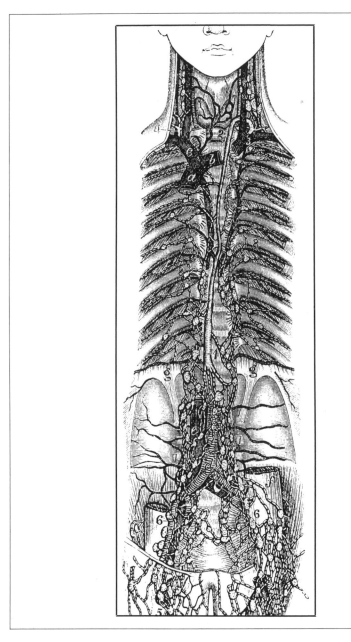

This 19th-century drawing of the lymphatic system, which helps the body fight infections, reveals how imperfectly the system was then understood. Ideas about the lymphatic system had to be extensively revised after Sabin's startling discoveries about it were proven correct in the early years of the 20th century.

FOUR

Professor of Medicine

In a ceremony held at Baltimore's Academy of Music in June 1900 and accompanied by the music of German composer Richard Wagner, Sabin graduated from medical school. At the age of 29, she was now ready to embark on the next stage of her career: serving as an intern. There were three openings for interns at the Hopkins Hospital, to be filled by the best students from the class of 1900. Sabin and another recent graduate, Dorothy Reed, were among the top contenders for the openings.

The hospital board did not want to fill two of its three positions with women, however. Sabin, who had a higher standing in school than Reed,

offered to turn down an intern position so Reed could have it. This infuriated Reed. "We both go, or forget it," she said.

Sabin decided to side with Reed, thereby supporting the feminist cause more publicly than ever before. She was not entirely comfortable with making any demands on the Hopkins Hospital. But when both women were awarded internships, Sabin felt gratified.

Before long, the issue of sexual discrimination arose again. After completing her internship in the required year, Sabin became eligible for a staff position at the Hopkins Hospital, except that the institution did not employ female physicians on its staff. Sabin steeled herself as the Women of Baltimore prepared to challenge this rule. Then Mall intervened: He offered Sabin a position in his lab. He had missed her during her internship and was convinced she had the ability to become a first-rate researcher. Upon learning of Mall's request, the Women of Baltimore provided Sabin with a fellowship amounting to $75 a month so she could afford to work with Mall.

From 1901 to 1902, Sabin pursued her work on lymphatics, further documenting her extraordinary findings that the system sprang from the blood vessels and that the endings of lymphatic channels were closed. She also took the first of many trips to Leipzig, Germany, to work at the university where Mall's mentors still taught. There, she arranged to have several three-dimensional models built from her atlas by an expert model maker.

During this period, Sabin made several significant friendships. The first was with Mall's wife, Mabel, who had also attended medical school and was the same age as Sabin. Now treated like a peer rather than a student, Sabin finally felt comfortable establishing close ties with her former professor's wife.

Sabin also formed a close friendship with Edith Houghton, a first-year medical student who had been an actor before coming to the Hopkins. An ardent feminist and a social reformer, Houghton fell in love with Donald Hooker, another medical student, and he, too, became friends with Sabin. Through Houghton, Sabin also met Dr. Mary Sherwood and Dr. Lillian Welsh, who had studied medicine in Europe and now practiced in Baltimore. Like Houghton, they were interested in social medicine, which benefited the disadvantaged. They were also active in an institution called the Evening Dispensary for Working Women and Girls. The dispensary was known for treating tuberculosis cases, and Sabin agreed to donate some of her time to its activities.

By the time Sabin had completed her fellowship, her research on lymphatics was considered so important that she was offered a professorship at the Hopkins. The school made no further fuss about her sex, even though it had never had a female professor before. As assistant professor of anatomy, Sabin took on a heavy teaching schedule. She conducted the first-year anatomy class and supervised the work of her students.

That same year, 1903, a series of Sabin's research papers on lymphatics was published. For the first time, her surprising thesis became widely known. Initially, Mall was not sure that he agreed with her findings. Yet he still had not discovered any mistakes in her research and therefore supported the publication of her papers. In time, he became convinced Sabin was right and defended her ideas to his German mentors, who doubted the accuracy of Sabin's conclusions. "The facts are correct and have been verified," Sabin

She Won $1000 Prize for Her Knowledge of Medicine

In 1903, Sabin won the Naples Table Fellowship, a $1,000 prize offered by the Association for the Promotion of Scientific Research by Women. The award helped Sabin gain a measure of fame and a high profile in the newspapers, but more importantly, it funded one of her many trips to Europe to keep up with the latest scientific developments.

Mount Vernon Square, where the Walters Art Gallery and the
Peabody Conservatory of Music are located, became one of Sabin's
favorite places to relax in Baltimore.

added confidently. "The reasoning is correct and has been justified."

Nearly 10 years later, Sabin's theories were proved correct in the Hopkins laboratories. But even in 1903, her work was considered solid enough to win a Naples Table Fellowship, which was sponsored by a group of American women who wished to enable a woman to study at the well-known research station in Naples, Italy, where many of the world-renowned German professors conducted research. The fellowship offered a $1,000 stipend and allowed Sabin to travel again to Europe.

Dividing her schedule between trips overseas, activities at the dispensary, work in the lab, and her teaching commitments, Sabin had little time left for socializing. It was convenient to maintain friendships among those with whom she shared her interest in research and medicine: the Malls, Houghton and Hooker, and others. Still, the Women of Baltimore wondered about Sabin's apparent lack of interest in marriage, and a rumor began to circulate that the gifted investigator was mourning a fiancé who had tragically died of typhoid fever.

Sabin did not deny the rumors, but in truth there had been no such man in her life. Although photographs show that she was a pretty child and an attractive young woman, Sabin believed herself plain. She thought that her hair was "too curly" and her hands "too small." She had little confidence in herself when it came to dealing with men in social situations, although she valued them as friends and as colleagues in the research lab. Moreover, Sabin believed that there was not enough room for both marriage and medicine in her life. She knew that other women successfully combined the two—Sabin herself wrote later that there was no reason for a married woman to give up her medical career. But for herself, the dedication with which she approached her work did not leave much room for romance.

In 1903, Sabin was rewarded with a promotion for her extraordinary devotion to her work. She was made associate professor of anatomy, and her salary was raised to the then generous figure of $2,500 a year. As an associate professor, she continued to labor at her investigations in the spacious, yellow-walled laboratories of the Hopkins. At Mall's instruction, the interior brick walls were painted a soft yellow, to yield a sense of light.

With her position at the university secure, Sabin decided it was time to find her own apartment. After several years in the Hen House, she had moved in with Gabrielle Clements, an art teacher. Clements's home was also her studio, and Sabin enjoyed living among her friend's work as well as the fine paintings Clements collected. But Sabin had lived in the homes of others since her mother's death; she had never had a home of her own. In 1903, she set about finding one.

A friend showed Sabin a pleasant walk-up apartment on Preston Street, near the medical school. Sabin rented it immediately and decorated it cheerfully, using plenty of yellow—still her

By 1910, Johns Hopkins Medical School had moved to its newly built campus, called Homewood. Sabin studied and taught there for more than 20 years.

favorite color. When her longtime friend Ella Denison visited Baltimore, bringing along clippings of plants from her own garden, Sabin was delighted. Vibrant red geraniums soon joined Sabin's irises in colorful window boxes.

By 1905, Sabin felt quite at home in Baltimore. Her favorite area of the city was Mount Vernon Square, where the Peabody Conservatory of Music and the Walters Art Gallery are located. She especially liked to visit the small gallery, gathering her thoughts while sitting across from the paintings of El Greco, a 16th-century Greek painter who worked in Spain.

There was usually little time for reflection, however. In 1905, Sabin's friend Edith Houghton graduated from medical school and married fellow graduate Donald Hooker. The newlyweds continued their interest in social medicine by setting up the St. George's Guild, a home for unwed mothers. The guild also provided treatment for and information about sexually transmitted diseases, more or less an unmentionable topic in turn-of-the-century Baltimore; Donald Hooker also gave lectures on these venereal diseases. Such actions outraged and offended many, but not the unflappable Sabin, who helped the Hookers with their guild work.

In addition to her growing artistic and social interests, Sabin continued to devote a great deal of time to her laboratory work and to teaching. The medical laboratories at the Hopkins, which had been designed by Franklin Paine Mall himself, were her home away from home. They were located in a three-story brick building named the Women's Memorial Fund Building, in recognition of the contribution of the Women of Baltimore. The third floor housed the dissecting rooms, amply lit by skylights. At Mall's insistence, these rooms were kept spotlessly clean, thus providing a contrast to most medical schools in the early 1900s, for the relationship between unsanitary conditions and disease had not yet been fully established. Mall kept up with the newest developments in bacteriology, however, and insisted that the laboratories' tables and floors be swabbed with ammonia each night. He also banned smoking in the dissecting rooms. Sabin noted that Mall was "a remarkable housekeeper," and she adopted his stringent hygienic standards for the rest of her career.

In this brightly lit, spotless environment, Sabin proved herself to be an exacting researcher. Her slides, with their carefully dyed specimens, were meticulously prepared, and she kept records of every microscope lens she ever ordered.

At first, Sabin's investigations were a continuation of her work on the lymphatic system. Her controversial theory was not definitively proved until 1920, when Hopkins scientists Eleanor Linten Clark and Elliot Clark observed the formations of lymphatic "sprouts" in the transparent tail of a newly hatched tadpole. Therefore, between 1905 and 1920 Sabin periodically had to gather evidence to support her earlier research.

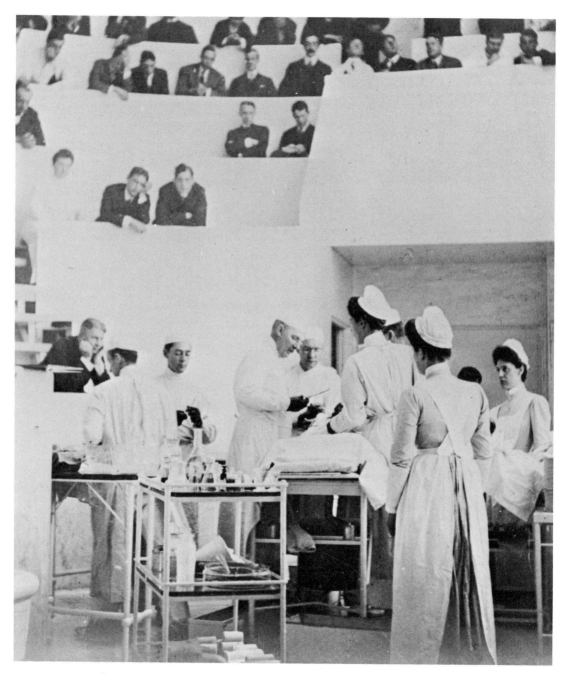

Students and faculty often observed surgical procedures in the operating theater at Johns Hopkins Hospital. Sabin was an associate in the anatomy department when this photograph was taken in 1903.

Engrossing as these investigations were, Sabin never lost interest in her job as teacher. In Sabin's mind, the two activities were closely connected. "All teachers should be engaged in research," she wrote. "Research lifts teaching to a higher plane." She also felt that teaching had a supreme dignity all its own. "What higher title could there be than that of great teacher?" Mall said, and Sabin agreed. She thought that medical and scientific advances depended on encouraging promising young researchers. Just as Mall had supported her early efforts, so she sought to inspire her own students.

Like Mall, Sabin felt that a student was his or her own best teacher; the professor's role was only to point the way. "The selection of a problem for a student needs nice judgment," Sabin explained. Mall had shown such judgment in assigning Sabin work on lymphatics and on the baby's brain. Sabin tried to do the same for her own students. Once a problem had been assigned, she withdrew to allow her students to work through their own discoveries. Sabin humorously explained her teaching method by saying, "Mall once told his wife, as he watched her bathe the baby, 'Why don't you just throw her in and let her work out her own technique?'"

Another way in which Sabin emulated Mall was by being remarkably generous. One of Mall's mentors, the German physiologist Carl Ludwig, once took rough notes and sketches Mall sent him from America and converted them into an article after having the sketches reworked by a professional artist. Ludwig then published the paper under Mall's name. Mall was astonished by this kindness and exceedingly grateful for it. His watchword became "Pass it on," and he passed on many of his findings to Sabin, who in turn passed them on to her students.

A dedicated teacher, Sabin spent many late hours in the lab, preparing slides and plates so her students could get directly to work in the morning and not get bogged down by these tasks. She always left the execution of experiments to them, so that they might experience the joy of discovery. And should a student make an original discovery, Sabin gave him or her credit, insisting that the work be published under the student's name. If the work was a joint effort and the student had done most of it—as was often the case—the published paper would bear two authors' names, with Sabin's appearing in the secondary position.

Sabin was a popular teacher in many respects. Although some students complained that her speaking style was dull, most found that Sabin's enthusiasm for her work, which allowed her to pursue a topic through a dense forest of detail, made her classes stimulating and fascinating. Her laboratory-based lectures were often attended by other professors eager to learn of the exciting developments taking place in Sabin's lab. This mark of esteem from her peers helped to dissolve Sabin's persistent shyness. Her confidence increased, and her teaching style grew more open and self-assured.

Sabin (second from left) and Dr. William Osler (third from left) flanked by two associates. Sabin had studied with the world-renowned Osler, whose teaching style and philosophy greatly influenced medical education. At the time, Sabin was beginning her career in Franklin Paine Mall's laboratory following her graduation from medical school.

FIVE

"The Special Fitness of Women"

After living at Preston Street for five years, Sabin moved twice within a short span in 1908, both times to apartments on Baltimore's Park Avenue. Each apartment was larger than the last and gave Sabin more space in which to entertain. A wonderful cook and gracious hostess, she liked to hold dinner parties for her students and colleagues. Well aware of her passion for exactitude, Sabin was not above poking fun at her work in the lab. In the kitchen, she would playfully make her students stand before her oven with a stopwatch, ready to turn the steaks she was preparing at precisely three minutes.

During this period, Sabin continued to make trips to Germany, especially to the University of Leipzig. She was always interested in learning the most advanced techniques for staining labo-ratory specimens, and these advances usually came from Leipzig. She made most of these trips during the summer, when school was not in session.

One such excursion took place in 1910, when Sabin and her sister sailed for Europe. Florence was especially cheerful during this voyage. A few days before the journey began, she had been awarded the first of the 17 honorary degrees she would receive during her life: a doctorate of science (Sc.D.) from her alma mater, Smith College.

In 1913, on another trip to Germany with her sister, Sabin had a particularly exhilarating stay at the laboratories in Leipzig. There she learned a brand-new technique that involved the use of "living" stains, which allowed one to work with live tissues. When injected into living tissue, these new stains interacted with it, producing an observable result. Sabin was excited about applying this new technique in her work.

During this trip, Sabin also undertook a mission for Franklin Paine Mall. To fill an opening at the Hopkins, he had asked her to recruit a European researcher able to "measure the human embryo with an adequate technique." Sabin found just the person in Dr. Michael Reichert, who came to Baltimore that fall. Sabin was so elated over her success with the new dyes and in convincing Reichert to come to the Hopkins that she wished to return immediately to Baltimore. But at her sister's request, she delayed her return and accompanied Mary on a walking tour in the Alps.

When Sabin finally returned to Baltimore, she experimented eagerly with her new stains. Attempting to stimulate vein growth in pig embryos, she stained live specimens of pig embryo with the living dye. Even though her results were inconclusive, in 1914 she published a paper that described her investigation.

When World War I broke out that same year, Sabin found herself in considerable turmoil. She had always admired Germany and deeply valued her research visits there, yet Germany was fast becoming the enemy of the United States. Moreover, Reichert was forced to return home to his native land, and the free-flowing exchange between Baltimore and Leipzig that had proved so fruitful came to a halt.

Above all, Sabin felt a deep aversion for the institution of war. "What a pitiful contrast do the sums we spend on teaching make with the sums we spend on war!" she lamented. Mall shared her views. Writing to a German colleague who questioned Sabin's lymphatics theory in 1915, he said, "I think Miss Sabin's discovery regarding the growth of lymphatics is one of the very greatest importance. It is an extremely small point, but has caused an immense amount of trouble for the past 200 years, and I am afraid when I go abroad again, we shall have to fight it out. But at any rate, this fighting will be more interesting than the present European war which seems to be so pointless."

Mall never made this trip to Germany to "fight it out" with his colleague. In 1917—a year before the war's end—he died, at the age of 55, after an operation for gallstones.

Mall's death left the chair of the head of the department of anatomy vacant. Sabin, who had worked with him for 20 years and had been sponsored by him above all others, was the logical choice as Mall's successor. But Sabin faced an uphill battle. No woman had ever chaired a department at the Hopkins. In addition, the department of anatomy was considered the most important department at the school, and the trustees were particularly reluctant to appoint a woman to head it. In the end, the position was given to a man who had once been one of Sabin's pupils.

The decision was so clearly unjust that Sabin's students, without consulting her, planned a large demonstration against it. Sabin, however, did not wish

*The outbreak of World War I disrupted the dialogue between
American and German scientists, which greatly upset both Sabin and
Franklin Paine Mall, who called the war "so pointless."*

to become the center of controversy. She believed that she was the right person for the post, yet she felt the issues in her case did not warrant such an extreme and public response. In her opinion, disappointment over her failure to be promoted was better handled with quiet good grace. When Sabin refused to support the demonstration, it quickly fizzled. Asked if she would stay on at the Hopkins, she said, "Of course I'll stay. I have research in progress."

Sabin was offered another chair instead—that of the department of histology (the study of blood). It was a lesser assignment, yet it still made her the first female to achieve a full professorship at the Hopkins. Sabin accepted the appointment graciously—along with its salary raise of $200 a year—but the episode had been painful for her. In fact, it was her first defeat in a career that had been characterized by one stunning success after another. It was all the more galling because it was due

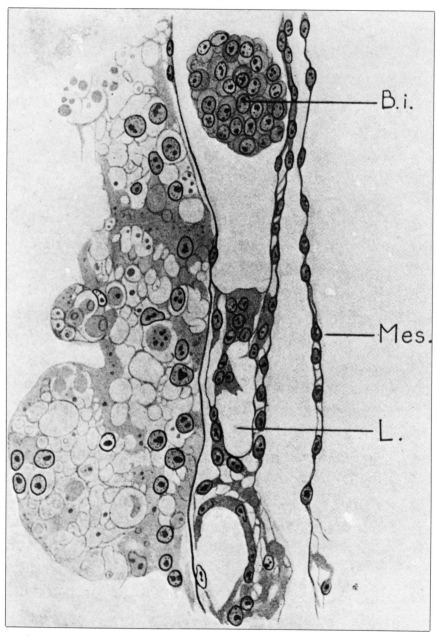

Sabin investigated the origin of blood vessels and cells after her findings about the lymphatic system gained wide acceptance. This early-20th-century diagram shows a blood islet (B.i.), the mesoderm (Mes.), and the lumen of a blood vessel (L.)—all important to the formation of blood cells.

only to discrimination on account of her sex. All her hard work and spectacular achievements were not enough to overcome the deeply entrenched prejudice against women in the mostly male medical hierarchy that ran Johns Hopkins.

Sabin swallowed her hurt feelings. As always, she buried herself in research, trying to work in a lab surrounded by reminders of the mentor she had lost. Even prosaic details saddened her. She wrote, "Our laboratory is full of examples of beautiful injections . . . blood vessels, cleared embryos . . . and many other [preparations left by Mall]." In 1918, she published a tribute to him in the popular medical journal *Science*.

Sabin's hard work began to pay off when she launched her most exciting investigation since the discovery of the origin of the lymphatic system. Having established that the lymphatics arose from the blood vessels by sprouts, she now became interested in endothelium, the substance from which the sprouts themselves developed. Of particular interest to Sabin was the growth of blood vessels and the origin of blood cells within the endothelium.

Using the live staining technique she had learned in Germany, Sabin stained the developing embryo of a chick and watched through her microscope as the first tiny blood vessels in the embryo formed from the endothelium. She stayed up all night to observe the first heartbeat of the chick, reflected in the pulsing of those earliest vessels. Sabin was so fascinated by what was taking

place on her slides that she did not even notice when dawn crept in the windows and light spread across the yellow laboratory walls. "It was the most exciting experience of my life," she said later. "To watch life begin!"

Although she could find laboratory work completely absorbing, Sabin was not blind to events in the world around her. In 1914, Edith Hooker, intent on expanding her efforts on behalf of women from the wards of the St. George's Guild into an active campaign for woman suffrage, founded the Just Government League of Maryland. In 1919, the group sponsored a letter-writing campaign to Congress to help win women the right to vote. For a period of one week, Sabin and Mabel Mall helped Hooker mail 10 letters per day to each of 130 legislators. Sabin handwrote 140 of these letters. Although they had no immediate effect, Hooker's league proved useful. Eventually, it was absorbed into the National Woman's Party, which became one of the most influential of the groups that finally succeeded in 1920 in gaining women the right to vote.

Although Sabin was basically a shy person who was not fond of drawing attention to herself, she was not afraid to speak out on matters that were extremely important to her. She was comfortable with donating her time to worthy women's causes and supporting the woman suffrage campaign. Yet others felt differently. After the letter-writing campaign, Sherwood and Welsh spoke to Sabin about how she could be of most use to the feminist

At the beginning of the 20th century, American women stepped up their efforts to gain the right to vote. Many of Sabin's friends were active in the burgeoning movement for woman suffrage, and Sabin herself took part in letter-writing campaigns and parades.

cause. They felt her prominence as a researcher set an inspiring example and did more for the cause of women than did her presence marching in a demonstration. (Sabin had marched in suffrage parades in both Baltimore and Washington, D.C.) Edith Hooker and Mabel Mall agreed, and Sabin, somewhat reluctantly, retired to her lab. Still, she proudly named her first automobile the *Susan B. Anthony*, after one of the most active fighters for woman suffrage and women's rights.

Sabin also carried on the battle by encouraging women to enter the field of medicine. "How glad I am to so affirm my profound faith in the special fitness of women for the medical profession!" she wrote in 1922. To critics who were skeptical about female research scientists, she replied tartly, "There are perhaps fewer women working on the scientific side of medicine, but no one would now advocate eliminating the work of a Madame Curie [the discoverer of radium] because of a prejudice against the sex of the worker." Sabin also cautioned against women giving up the practice of medicine once they married. "English women have been able to carry on the practice of medicine after marriage," she noted, "and it is quite possible to do."

In 1922, Sabin had the honor of introducing Marie Curie as a speaker to the American Association of University Women, a powerful women's lobbying group that worked for educational and social reform. Curie's work on radioactivity had won her and her husband, Pierre, the 1903 Nobel Prize in physics. Marie Curie won the prize again in 1911, this time in chemistry, making her the only person ever to be awarded the prize in both fields. Sabin, who admired Curie enormously, was deeply moved when she met the famed scientist.

In the same year, Sabin was invited to China to address the Peking Medical Union. She delivered a paper in Peking on the origins of blood cells and also advised the Chinese on the malaria epidemic they were then fighting. She suggested that China would be wiser to eradicate the mosquito that carried the disease than to spend money importing quinine. Sabin would continue throughout her life to argue that prevention is more important than treatment.

While in Peking, Sabin also bought several valuable Chinese paintings, thus beginning an extensive collection of Oriental art. When she returned to Baltimore, Gertrude Stein and her brother, Leo, who were among the most prominent and progressive art collectors of their day, heard of Sabin's purchases and were intrigued by the paintings. The Steins, who were also known for their sophisticated writings and unconventional attitudes, befriended Sabin and offered to advise her on future acquisitions.

Gertrude Stein, a controversial writer whose unusual prose style was characterized by virtually no punctuation, had in fact attended the Hopkins Medical School at the same time Sabin had. Gertrude Stein had also studied

Sabin's purchases of Chinese paintings sparked the interest of writer and art patron Gertrude Stein, who introduced Sabin to a broad and varied social circle in Baltimore. Stein later moved to Paris, where this photograph was taken.

under Mall and had been assigned by him the task of constructing a model from Sabin's atlas of the baby's brain. Stein was such a poor technician, however, that her model collapsed and had to be thrown out.

Nevertheless, Stein had impressed Mall, who respected her independent spirit. Shy, studious Florence Sabin had also admired Stein's colorful personality, and in 1922 the two women resumed their acquaintance. The Steins invited Sabin to the opera and introduced her to their wide and cultured circle of friends.

In 1922, a new field of research opened up to Sabin as well. She began to focus on the discovery of the origins and functions of white blood cells known as monocytes. These large cells with their tiny nuclei are particularly significant in mobilizing the body's defense against infection. Sabin's interest was piqued by the potential role of the monocyte in warding off tuberculosis, an infection primarily of the respiratory system—although it can attack other parts of the body.

By the 1920s, tuberculosis had reached epidemic proportions in the United States. It was the single highest cause of death among all age groups. Sabin's earlier research was of importance in understanding how various body systems and structures are formed and perpetuate themselves, but the social relevance of her work was less immediate. Because the work with monocytes had greater practical relevance, Sabin found the new research even more satisfying. It occupied her

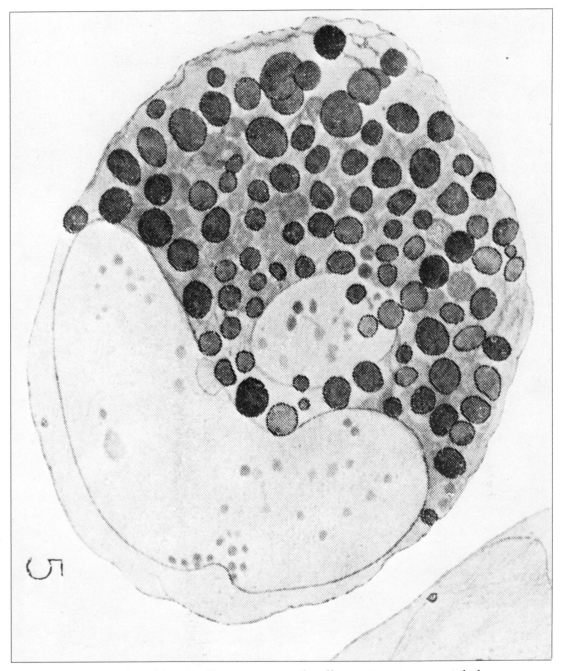

A sketch of blood cells was among the illustrations in an article by Sabin entitled "Studies of Living Human Blood-Cells," published in the Bulletin of Johns Hopkins Hospital *in October 1923.*

This 1924 publicity photograph of Sabin was distributed to the national press with the note that she was "the only woman who has been admitted to our National Academy of Science." Two decades passed before another woman was elected to this influential body.

for the rest of her days as an investigator.

Sabin did not carry out this research at the Hopkins, however. In 1924 and 1925, she received three striking honors. First, she was named president of the American Society of Anatomists, the most distinguished professional organization in her field, and became the first woman to be honored with the presidency. Second, she was elected to membership in the National Academy of Sciences, again the first woman to be so recognized. In fact, Madame Curie had failed to be elected to the corresponding French body solely because she was a woman. Moreover, no other women would be elected to the National Academy of Sciences for another 20 years.

The third honor brought far-reaching implications. In the fall of 1925, Sabin was offered a position at New York's newly founded Rockefeller Institute for Medical Research. At that point, Sabin had lived in Baltimore for 28 years, and the decision to leave for New York was a difficult one. But after she decided to accept the position at the Rockefeller Institute, she began to look forward to the move, even though it would mean giving up teaching in favor of pure research.

Sabin spent her last afternoon in Baltimore walking through Mount Vernon Square and her other favorite neighborhoods. Then she visited the Walters Art Gallery, where she sat among the paintings by El Greco. In moving to New York, she would be leaving many old friends behind.

While he was the director of the Rockefeller Institute, Dr. Simon Flexner attracted a world-renowned research staff. A gifted investigator himself, he identified the dysentery bacillus, developed a serum to treat meningitis, and directed the research team that identified the virus that causes polio.

SIX

The Rockefeller Years

Soon after a front-page column in the *Baltimore Sun* announced her departure from the Hopkins, 53-year-old Florence Sabin closed down her laboratory, packed up her Spencer microscope, and moved to New York. It was the fall of 1925, and the leaves in Central Park were just beginning to change. Sabin's new apartment, on East 80th Street, near Lexington Avenue, was more spacious and elegant than her Baltimore walk-ups had been. But most important to her was that it was within walking distance of both Central Park, where she planned to resume her habit of taking nature walks, and her new job at the Rockefeller Institute for Medical Research.

The institute (currently called Rockefeller University) is located at 66th Street and York Avenue, in a tall limestone building overlooking the East River. Although the institute was barely 20 years old in 1925, it had already become one of the foremost research centers in the world, known especially for its work in the sphere of infectious disease.

Back in 1901, an adviser to philanthropist John D. Rockefeller, Sr., read a medical book that ignited his interest. The book was by Dr. William Osler, physician in chief of the Hopkins Hospital in Sabin's student days. Osler's book was for the general reader. Simple and straightforward, it presented Osler's plea that more attention and money be devoted to medical research. Through graphic descriptions of disease and dramatic prose, it told why research deserved support. The vivid book so impressed Rockefeller's adviser that he convinced the philanthropist to donate a quarter of a million dollars to found an institute dedicated solely to medical research.

One of Osler's pupils—and a star at the Hopkins in his own day—was appointed to head the new institute. This was Dr. Simon Flexner, who had been Sabin's pathology professor at the Hopkins. Flexner, who was from a poor family in Louisville, Kentucky, had two brothers who had attained as high a position in their field as Flexner had in his. Abraham Flexner specialized in education and became the first director of the Institute for Advanced Study in Princeton, New Jersey. Bernard Flexner was a New York criminal lawyer, considered to have one of the finest legal minds of his day.

Between 1901 and Sabin's arrival in 1925, Simon Flexner had steered the Rockefeller Institute in exciting and innovative directions. He had been instructed by his board to employ only the most brilliant scientists. "Only a genius is worth a laboratory wing," one member told him.

"Genius" was exactly how Flexner described Florence Sabin. She had been his student at the Hopkins, and he had admired her even then. After all, the work she had done in lymphatics while still a student had upset the theories of medical scholars at the finest European universities. Another project of her student days had been published as a textbook that was still considered the authority in its area. Moreover, she was performing significant research on the monocyte, a cell that was known to be important but was little understood. In Flexner's view, Sabin was "the most eminent of all living women scientists," and he considered her recruitment a real coup.

Back at the Hopkins, Sabin's departure was considered a blow of corresponding measure. Many of her students later followed her to New York. The first to do so was Dr. Charles A. Doan, who arrived in 1925 and remained for five years. He was followed by a long line of others, who sometimes worked simultaneously (one, Dr. James R. Cash, worked without pay as a volunteer for two years) and sometimes alone with Sabin. Most stayed several years before accepting senior posts elsewhere.

Sabin moved busily about, setting up her new labs. They were sunny and bright, just as Mall's laboratories at the Hopkins had been, and they were kept just as scrupulously clean. In fact, Sabin's concern with cleanliness had become almost a fetish. She had always washed her hands between each stage of experimentation and upon entering and leaving the lab. Now these procedures became mandatory.

Yet Sabin was never so rigid that her lab became an unfriendly place. The atmosphere, if spotless, was also congenial and always filled with the excitement and energy of discovery. One of her co-workers at the Rockefeller Institute wrote: "Dr. Sabin was one of those people who, however strenuous the previous day might have been, waked at the crack of dawn with great enthusiasm for what the day was to hold. She was nearly always the first one at the laboratory, and greeted every one with

The building on the left, part of what is now Rockefeller University, was named Simon Flexner Hall in memory of the institute's first director. Sabin spent 13 years conducting research at its laboratories.

Dr. James R. Cash followed Sabin from Johns Hopkins to the Rockefeller Institute. His devotion to research was so great that he worked there without pay for two years.

a *joie de vivre* [joy of living] which started the day pleasantly for all of us."

In her new lab, Sabin began by picking up where she had left off at the Hopkins with her work on the monocyte cell. Her monocyte studies had piqued Flexner's interest many years back, for Flexner himself was conducting research on the body's humoral defenses against disease. (A humoral defense refers to the body's secretion of fluids to combat a disease-causing agent: An example is the way one's nose runs when one is suffering from a cold—the draining fluids carry out harmful bacteria with them.) Flexner felt it would be useful to combine his research with investigations of the body's cellular response to disease, which included the functioning of monocytes. It was one more reason why he had been eager to have Sabin join his staff.

Earlier, in Baltimore, Sabin had noticed that the large monocyte cells she studied under her microscope seemed, when confronted by the tubercle bacillus (the bacteria that causes tuberculosis), to have a role in combating them. She decided to test further the idea that monocytes were important to the body's defense against tuberculosis. To do so, she took a tubercle (tubercular lesion) and extracted its various chemical components—its fractions. She was able to extract lipids (groups of fats), waxes (substances composed of fatty acids), polysaccharides (complex sugars), and proteins, among other compounds.

Each of these fractions, when injected back into a healthy lab animal, provoked a distinct and different reaction in terms of the body's defense against it. Lipids, for instance, produced monocytes. Waxes caused fibrous tissue to grow. A particular type of fat caused tissue and blood cells to grow rapidly. The polysaccharide fraction attracted leukocytes (small, colorless cells) but then seemed to kill them. The proteins caused fever.

Of all these responses, Sabin considered the response to the lipids—the formation of monocytes—to be the most significant. This was a controversial idea, because Flexner believed the humoral responses were more important, and others held differing opinions. Still, Sabin's findings were greeted with some excitement at the institute.

In 1926, Sabin joined the newly formed research committee of the National Tuberculosis Association, which coordinated all tuberculosis research done in the United States, including that carried out by pharmaceutical companies, the producers of medicines. Information, money, and research facilities were all shared so that the dreaded disease might be conquered as quickly as possible. Indeed, by the 1960s tuberculosis had dropped from first to 18th as the chief cause of death in the United States. Sabin's tuberculosis research helped pave the way for this decline.

A second phase of Sabin's research, begun a few years after she joined the National Tuberculosis Association's research committee, involved work with antibodies, substances that the body produces in response to disease. Although in the 1920s investigators were aware of antibodies, they were uncertain which cells produced them. Sabin believed it was the monocytes that accepted antigens, the agents that stimulate antibodies into action; thus, the monocytes were the cells where antibodies formed.

To prove her theory, Sabin resumed using the dyes that she had studied in Germany and perfected at the Hopkins. A new dark red dye that had antigen properties had recently been discovered. Sabin injected this dye into monocyte cells and found that she was able to watch the formation of antibodies reacting to the dye's "invasion." She concluded that she had been correct in perceiving that antibodies were born in the monocyte cell.

Sabin now knew where antibodies arose and what stimulated them to form, but she still did not know precisely what they were. Were they made from material "donated" by the invader antigen, for instance? Sabin was to work on this problem for the rest of her research years.

Today, the questions Sabin addressed in her research are still not fully answered. When effective treatments for tuberculosis were found some 20 years later, the new drugs did not require an in-depth understanding of monocytes or antibodies. Nevertheless, her work on monocytes still stands, whereas many conflicting theories have been discarded. Sabin said earlier, "New concepts are often ignored because the age in which they appear is not sufficiently advanced to comprehend them." Such a statement applies to her work with the monocytes. Although her theories were not ignored, they were so far in advance of most research done in the 1920s and 1930s that they were not always fully appreciated.

In conducting research of this high caliber, Sabin retained her generosity and fair-mindedness toward those with whom she worked. She continued to "pass it on." Although Doan and his successors were no longer her students, they worked under her direction. Sabin still allowed each scientist to carry out his or her own research, to make his or her own discoveries and to receive credit for them. She published many joint papers with her colleagues and continued her practice of having her name receive second billing if the work was mainly done by her associate. If Sabin did not feel her own contribution was sufficient, the associate's name appeared alone.

Sabin's name not only appeared in scientific journals. With ample funding and the concentration of talent at institutional research centers leading to exciting scientific breakthroughs, the general public began to pay attention to the discoveries of research scientists, who were learning more and more about fighting deadly diseases and uncovering the mysteries of the human body. As Sabin and her team proceeded with their investigations and reported their findings back to the research committee, a number of popular magazine and newspaper writers devoted articles

Sabin (front row, second from left) poses with her research team in June 1933. She not only conducted research of the highest quality but also maintained a friendly and collegial atmosphere in the laboratory.

to an explanation of developments at the Rockefeller Institute.

As Sabin's name became well known to interested readers, she began to receive volumes of mail. Letters came not only from researchers and colleagues but from tuberculosis sufferers and their relatives, who begged her for help. She always answered these letters as informatively and as kindly as possible, even though her research remained on a plane too theoretical to be of immediate use. "I am sorry to say that I know nothing concerning the cure for tuberculosis reported in the clipping which you enclosed" was her typical response.

In 1928, Sabin became involved with another project close to her heart. The National Academy of Sciences assigned her the task of compiling Franklin Paine Mall's biography. It was an academy tradition that after a member's death, an essay-length biography of that person was written by a living academy member. Sabin was the logical choice to serve as Mall's biographer.

The project attracted so much interest, however, that Sabin was soon approached by a publisher, who asked her to expand the essay into a full-length book. Sabin agreed to do so. But in her usual thorough fashion, she took the task quite seriously. She had Simon Flexner, Donald Hooker, and others look over each draft of the manuscript. When Flexner told Sabin that she had not quite captured the spirit of Mall, she threw out what she had written and began all over again. Five years passed before she finished writing the book.

Upon the work's completion, Sabin was hospitalized for bursitis of the arm, an inflammation that she had acquired while typing the manuscript. Later, she developed pneumonia and blamed it on the strain that authorship caused. She vowed never to write another book, and she never did.

Nevertheless, the effort Sabin put into perfecting *Franklin Paine Mall: The Story of a Mind* was widely appreciated. In fact, the book was so well regarded that of the 50 reviews it received, not a single one was negative. Simon Flexner, who reviewed the book, called it "thorough" and "vivid." Mary Beard, who, with her husband, Charles, wrote extensively on American history, called the book "fascinating," and the dean of the University of Wisconsin wrote, "I have just finished reading your biography of Mall. I congratulate you on an extraordinary accomplishment. It is no reflection of my previous estimate of your abilities if I call it surprisingly good. From a literary point of view you could not have done better had you been a professional writer of biographies."

Taking a traditional approach at first, the biography traces Mall's roots through many generations to his ancestors who were farmers in Germany, then details his medical studies in Germany under the renowned physicians William His, professor of anatomy at the University of Leipzig, and Carl Ludwig, professor of physiology at that university. When Sabin covered the later periods of Mall's life, she took a new tack, delving into Mall's personal history in terms of his intellect. Sabin wrote:

> Ludwig was a masterly technician; he was resourceful, careful, inventive, and extremely skilled with his hands. Mall, I think, was less hand-minded naturally, yet he learned to work expertly. Mall was a thinker. It was often said of him that he would think for hours in order to plan the best possible way to do a thing, rather than to work by trial and error.

She went on to delve into her mentor's mind, exploring his thoughts, his theories, and his teaching methods.

When Sabin finally finished the biography, which was published in 1934, she had more time for her friends, which included many old acquaintances. Among these was Ned Sheldon, Ella Denison's nephew, who was one of the children Sabin had taken on nature walks in Wisconsin. Sheldon went on to Harvard and then became one of America's foremost playwrights. In 1929, when he was 38, he was stricken by an illness that was never precisely diagnosed. Yet it caused him to go blind within two years and later completely paralyzed him. He could still hear, however, and although he spent his last 15 years in bed, he was still able to work.

A parade of popular theater performers, including Helen Hayes, Katharine Cornell, and John Barrymore, visited Sheldon regularly after he became paralyzed. But his favorite guest was Florence Sabin, with whom he liked to discuss theater, books, and daily events. The morning after one of Sabin's visits, he sent her the following note:

> I seem to have worked hard in my sleep all night, though it was nevertheless restful sleep, for this morning I awoke with a clear plan for a new and I think good discussion of my paper. I felt mortified to think how I had revealed my fatigue to you, and the poor work which it had led to, but it was your faith and encouragement that waked up my mind. You can never know what a wonderful inspiration you are. I never came away from an evening with you without a feeling of deep joy.

Among Sabin's newly won friends, the most notable was Albert Einstein. Abraham Flexner brought Einstein to the Institute for Advanced Study in 1933, and the German-born physicist liked the institute so well that he said, "I am fire and flame about it." Flexner often gave small dinner parties attended by Einstein, and he invited Sabin to some of them. One evening, she was seated right next to Einstein, who was dressed in his usual rumpled fashion. Over the course of the evening, she was delighted to find that one of the century's top minds was, she later said, "utterly simple, as all great thinkers are." She wrote to her sister, "His laugh rings out and makes everyone around him happy."

Sabin wrote frequently to her sister, often telling her ordinary bits of information. In one typical interchange,

Sabin met the noted physicist Albert Einstein several times in the 1930s at dinner parties held by Simon Flexner's brother Abraham, who headed the Institute for Advanced Study at Princeton, New Jersey.

which took place in 1932, 63-year-old Mary wrote to Florence that while traveling by automobile she had "stopped at an auto court before it got dark, at 7." Florence wrote back that the ache in her arm (from typing her book) had subsided.

Sabin's life began to take a more exciting turn after the University in Exile was founded in New York in 1933. Later called the New School for Social Research, it was originally established to relocate talented German professors who were being prosecuted or hampered in their research by German chancellor Adolf Hitler's Nazi party, which came to power in March 1933. Many, but not all, of the professors who joined the New School's faculty were Jewish, for although Hitler particularly targeted Jews for discrimination—and eventual extermination—he dismissed thousands of men and women of all faiths from their university posts when he felt threatened by their beliefs. The University in Exile gave the finest of these professors a new and enlightened place to work.

Sabin served as a member of the university's board from 1936 to 1938 and did much more than attend meetings. She actively sought positions of all types for the German refugee scholars. Albert Einstein once wrote to her, asking if she could find a position for a friend of his whose work required proximity to a cyclotron, a powerful apparatus that can energize nuclear particles. Sabin made a few inquiries and then wrote back with a list of

institutions that possessed this ultramodern piece of equipment. Sabin was actually flattered by Einstein's request; she liked the prominent physicist and was delighted to help him out.

Sabin herself needed little help. By 1938, she had received honorary degrees from the University of Michigan (1926), New York University (1933), Wilson College (1933), Syracuse University (1934), Oglethorpe University (1935), the University of Colorado (1935), the University of Pennsylvania (1935), and Russell Sage College (1938). Each of these schools awarded her a doctorate of science. In 1931, Goucher College also presented her with a doctorate of law.

Other honors that were heaped on Sabin were a $5,000 annual Achievement Award sponsored by *Pictorial Review* magazine in 1929; being selected by *Good Housekeeping* (via a nationwide poll) as one of the 12 most eminent women in the country in 1931; inclusion in 1935 on a list of the nation's 10 most outstanding women; and, in 1938, a $5,000 prize for excellence in scientific research in honor of M. Carey Thomas, one of the Women of Baltimore.

In 1938, Sabin was also actively pursuing her research on antibodies. She felt she was on the verge of a major discovery and was very absorbed in her work. Yet she was going on 67 years old and recognized that she should consider retirement. She firmly believed it was necessary to make way for younger researchers. Besides, projects on the verge of a breakthrough had a way of taking years to complete. Perhaps it was time to give up her wing at the Rockefeller Institute to another "genius."

Sabin made a quick decision: She would retire. Upon announcing her decision, she was immediately made an emeritus fellow by the Rockefeller Institute's director, who urged her to return to the institute and use the labs whenever she liked. But Sabin had decided to return to Colorado. There she would make a home with Mary, who had retired as a teacher in the Denver public school system.

Sabin with Bryn Mawr College president Marian Edwards Park and former Rockefeller Institute director Simon Flexner at a 1935 gathering to celebrate Bryn Mawr College's 50th anniversary. Sabin also received the M. Carey Thomas Award and its accompanying $5,000 prize during the festivities.

From 1936 to 1938, Sabin served on the board of the New York–based University in Exile and proved instrumental in finding teaching positions for many of the European scholars who were forced to flee Nazi Germany.

On the eve of Sabin's departure from New York, 40 of her friends threw a surprise dinner party for her at the Rainbow Room in Rockefeller Center. The president of Johns Hopkins University, as well as many others, praised her scientific work and skill in a series of speeches. Sabin replied with a speech of her own, made up on the spot, thanking them for the dinner and professing how much she loved her work.

Shortly thereafter, Sabin set off for Denver. She was not in an upbeat mood, however, for she was filled with considerable apprehension. She was not at all sure that she would like being retired. As she quickly found out, she did not enjoy it one bit.

When Sabin retired from the Rockefeller Institute at the age of 67, she was still a vibrant woman with years of productive work ahead of her.

SEVEN

"Retired"

Upon returning to Denver in 1939, Florence Sabin worked hard, as was her fashion, only this time it was at the business of being retired. She did not find retired life all that enjoyable. For one thing, her sister, Mary, proved to be unenthusiastic about their setting up a home together. Florence remained firm on this issue, however, and the sisters rented an apartment on the first floor of a new building near lush Cheesman Park.

It was Mary Sabin's fantasy that when Florence retired, she would involve herself in Mary's favorite activities: attending meetings of the Colonial Dames, a patriotic organization requiring that one have ancestors from the colonial period, and participating in the Colorado Mountain Club, which Mary had helped found in 1912 and which by then boasted several hundred members. Mary knew that she and Florence shared an interest in hiking that dated back to their childhood. But Florence showed no real interest in taking part in these activities.

Sabin seemed to brighten up only after she was asked by Dr. Herbert Gasser, director of the Rockefeller Institute, to prepare a paper on the last five years of her research there. She immediately dropped everything, including whatever social plans Mary had made, and wrote the report. Shortly afterward, Florence Sabin returned to New York to complete a segment of the research she had been engaged in when she retired from the Rockefeller Institute.

Sabin also headed east to attend several board meetings. The John Simon Guggenheim Memorial Foundation, which was set up by Senator Simon Guggenheim in 1922 to honor one of his sons who had died as a young man, had invited her to join its advisory board. The foundation provided generous fellowships each year to scholars, writers, and artists at the pinnacle of their professions. As a board member, Sabin was expected to help select who would receive the lucrative grants. She also served on the boards of both the Rockefeller Institute and the Institute for Advanced Study and planned to attend their board meetings as well.

When Sabin arrived by train in New York, she emerged from Grand Central Station to find herself "back among good newspapers, soft water, and work." When she attended the Guggenheim board meeting, she found herself impressed with the application of Muriel Rukeyser, a distinguished poet, novelist, and biographer who began

Dr. Herbert Spencer Gasser, who was serving as director of the Rockefeller Institute when Sabin retired in 1938. Gasser valued her work so much that he asked Sabin to return to New York and write a paper summarizing her last years of research work.

publishing her work in the 1930s, and supported her for a fellowship. Rukeyser received a grant and, in the process, became a friend of Sabin's.

When Sabin visited her old labs, she found them completely cleaned out and not yet reassigned. Assigned someone else's lab to work in, she managed to complete her research project, which was on antibody formation in reaction to red antigen dye, and published the results. Energized by her work, Sabin returned reluctantly to Colorado. But her spirits rose quickly upon her arrival: Two research scientists from the University of Colorado, Dr. Ward Darley and Dr. Dumont Clark, asked for her help in their white blood cell research. Sabin began to frequent the university's laboratories, where she felt right at home.

Sabin kept herself busy in other ways as well. She had once been invited to join the Fortnightly Club, a philosophical society founded years earlier by Ella Denison, and she now decided to do so. Not content merely to attend club meetings, she wrote a paper, "On Humanism," for the club journal. Then her sister, Mary, who had traveled by herself to Alaska in 1935, when Florence was too busy to go, insisted on a return trip. Florence went reluctantly but wound up having a wonderful time.

Despite the fact that she was now leading a busy life in Colorado, Sabin looked forward to her next trip east. When the time came, she labored until late at night in the Rockefeller Institute labs, continuing her long search to un-

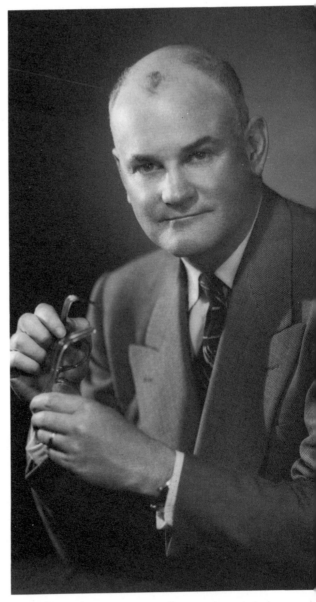

Upon Sabin's return to her native state in 1938, Dr. Ward Darley (shown here), of the University of Colorado Health Sciences Center, joined Dr. Dumont Clark in asking her to help with their white blood cell research.

derstand antibody formation. She eventually wound up publishing another paper on the topic.

As Sabin entered her seventies, she set up a pattern of traveling east for a short spell, then returning to the West, where she held meetings, lectures, and laboratory sessions. Although she continued to produce research papers—including a follow-up of her work on cellular reactions to fractions from the tubercle bacilli, which was published in 1941—this way of life left her unsatisfied. She felt she was being pulled in too many directions.

Nevertheless, Sabin could not stop herself from taking on new projects. In 1941, she became a member of the advisory committee on United China Relief, an organization that aided the starving, suffering Chinese in their effort to withstand famine as well as to resist the Japanese, who occupied China during World War II. Sabin had been interested in China ever since her speaking engagement there in 1921. In addition, she was invited to work on a variety of government committees.

In 1942, Sabin joined the board of the Children's Hospital in Denver. She was soon elected vice-president of the board. Although she was unable to attend most board meetings, she nonetheless tried to initiate new policies. It was at about this time that Sabin began to realize how poor the state of public health was in Colorado.

Her own health remained robust, though. She met with artist Lewis Schmidt, who had illustrated some of her articles, and asked him to design for her a bookplate. For this sticker containing Sabin's name, which she pasted into her books, Lewis came up with a drawing of a microscope, below which was inscribed Sabin's personal motto: "Thou O God, dost sell unto us all good things at the price of labor."

When asked about this quote years later, Sabin explained that it came from the artist Leonardo da Vinci and that she regarded it as the key to her success. "My secret," she said, "is workable for every man and woman. It is belief in and practice of that creed."

This "secret" made it impossible for Sabin to retire completely. Yet all her hard work during her retirement years left her frustrated, for she was struck by having a lack of focus, especially compared to what she had done in the past. Dissatisfied with how she was going about things, she began to turn down requests to give talks and to join boards. In her free time, she climbed Longs Peak, the highest mountain in Colorado's Estes Park, with her sister. But such a feat did little to soothe Florence's restlessness.

Soon, an opportunity to focus her efforts arrived from an unlikely quarter. In 1944, an outspoken journalist from the *Denver Post*, Frances Wayne, challenged Colorado's governor, John Vivian, to appoint a woman to his postwar planning commission. As World War II drew to a close, Vivian was running for reelection and did not want lose anyone's support. "Who would you suggest?" the governor asked.

Frances Wayne, nicknamed Pinky, was the forthright journalist who told Colorado governor John Vivian that he needed to appoint a woman to his administration and that the right person for the post was Florence Sabin.

When Governor Vivian gave Sabin a spot on his postwar planning commission in 1944, he had no idea she would prove a vigorous reformer whose efforts would contribute to his defeat in the 1946 gubernatorial election.

"Florence Sabin, of course," Wayne replied.

Vivian inquired about Sabin and learned that she had impressive credentials. She was also rather shy and elderly—someone unlikely to cause trouble. Uneager to have outspoken reformers in his administration, Vivian offered the distinguished doctor a position on his commission. After Sabin accepted, Vivian told her how happy he was to have her on board. Sabin smiled sweetly at this remark, prompting a grin from the governor, who was actually smirking at his own cleverness.

It did not take very long, though, for Vivian to discover that he had grossly underestimated Sabin's character.

With her wire-rimmed glasses and gray hair tied neatly in a bun, Sabin maintained a demure appearance in her later years. In reality, she was a whirlwind of activity and worked tirelessly to push public health bills through the Colorado legislature.

EIGHT

A Third Career

One day in 1949, as Florence Sabin stood before a mobile X-ray unit in Denver, trying to persuade her fellow citizens to have a free X ray taken as a preventive measure against the spread of tuberculosis, a reporter looked at her closely and inquired, "Are you really 78?" Amused by the question, Sabin responded, "Of course I'm 78."

The reporter then asked Sabin for the secret of her health and success. "Labor," she replied. "Labor is not a grinding ordeal to which one is driven by the whip of necessity. It's a privilege. Whether work means digging ditches, driving a car, or working for world understanding, it will keep you healthy and young if you work with enjoyment.

It's resistance to work—not work itself—that ages people."

"I see," said the reporter, clearly having heard more than he had expected. Then he started to ask another question, but Sabin was already helping a young medical technician usher a volunteer toward the X-ray equipment. It became obvious to the reporter that Sabin was not one to resist work.

Governor John Vivian had not immediately realized that fact. For political reasons of his own, he had not wanted the new chair of the health committee to advocate change and reform. Having appointed Sabin to the health committee in 1944, he turned his attention to other matters, confident that Sabin would not take her new appointment all that seriously. What the governor had not counted on was that Sabin was eager to plunge into new work for the public good and anxious to restore the focus she felt her life had lost. The Committee on Health was now her principal concern.

Having first discerned the sobering reality of health conditions in Colorado when she joined the Children's Hospital board of directors two years earlier, Sabin decided to research the health situation further. As she did so, she became horrified. Colorado had one of the highest disease rates and worst sanitation systems in the country. This combination promoted needless suffering and an unusually high death rate. According to her calculations, only 10 cents per person per year was allotted to public health in Colorado.

Sabin set out to remedy this situation as best she could. Publicizing the problem became her immediate priority. Her first act as chair of the health committee was to build a broad base of powerful backers. Accordingly, Sabin organized a series of dinner parties at Denver's luxurious Brown's Palace Hotel and invited Colorado's leaders in medicine, finance, and business to these affairs. She hoped to convince her guests that forceful and immediate action was essential to solving some of their fellow citizens' health problems.

When her guests were seated, Sabin addressed them with characteristic enthusiasm. She took pains not to accuse by name the officials she considered negligent, for that would have created an air of animosity and proved counterproductive. Instead, she explained that three-quarters of those who died in Colorado could have been saved, if only preventive health measures had been taken.

Sabin listed the diseases that were the biggest problems and discussed how each one could be fought. She covered the high tuberculosis rate and the waste of livestock due to brucellosis. She pointed out how Colorado produce was shunned in other states. She spoke graphically of bubonic plague, infant deaths, filthy milk, and polluted streams. Her audience was spellbound.

Those who had attended out of obligation, expecting a dull evening, were enchanted by the spirited doctor who spoke so convincingly. "She's the only hen medic I'd listen to for an hour," one of them remarked. It was not long before Sabin had swung opinion to her side and amassed the financial support needed to begin her work.

Sabin's plan for action was simple and effective. In essence, she tackled the problem by applying the scientific method she used in her laboratory work. Having been asked a lot of questions at the dinner meetings, she decided to research every question to which she did not know the answer. Her investigations raised new questions, and she checked into these as well. When she had finished her thorough inquiry, she made an appointment with a state legislator who shared her interest in public health. The gov-

During her later years in Colorado, Sabin spent much of her time conducting a grass-roots campaign among Colorado citizens. But she was also known to lobby lawmakers in the state capitol.

ernment official invited one of his colleagues to join them, and the three worked together to draft a series of bills designed to correct the crisis conditions Sabin had uncovered.

These pieces of legislation became known as both the Sabin program and the Sabin bills. There were six bills in all. They concerned funding hospital construction with federal money, reorganizing the state health department, changing the state health districts so that poorer counties could share resources, providing for the establish-

Although brucellosis was a disease that could sharply reduce the productivity of a dairy herd, Colorado's dairymen feared the cost of implementing preventive measures spelled out in the so-called Cow Health Bill sponsored by Sabin.

ment and funding of a state tuberculosis hospital, and increasing free health care for tuberculosis patients who were poor. The sixth bill was the most important to Sabin. It became known as the Cow Health Bill and provided for strict control of bru-cellosis, which infected almost half the cattle in Colorado and caused serious illnesses among consumers of meat and dairy products.

Sabin then had her friends submit the bills to a vote in the legislature, which, she knew, had a poor record for passing health bills. Many of the legislators received financial support from the milk and cattle industries, which opposed any measures against brucellosis that might cost them money. Sabin decided not to let such politics stop her. If she wanted her bills to pass, she would have to take them directly to the people.

And so she did. Day after day, often in the company of other state officials, such as Herbert Moe, Sabin toured Colorado and told the people what she had learned about health conditions in the state. In the National Academy of Sciences biography published after her death, the authors described how "this stocky, indomitable, sincere, honest, knowledgeable, and famous elderly woman scientist . . . caught the fancy of the public."

Sabin's approach in addressing farmers and laborers was always the same. It was the approach she had learned from Mall and had applied throughout her career: Present the facts, and allow the student (or citizen) to decide on the appropriate action. She also owed her lecture style to Mall. On the other hand, the methods that she applied in her stirring public campaign were derived from the Baltimore suffragists of the 1910s and 1920s and early social reformers such as her old friend Edith Hooker. No longer absorbed in lab work, Sabin was able to carry on her cause with unprecedented singlemindedness.

In county after county, Coloradans filled the schoolhouses, auditoriums, and women's clubs where Sabin spoke. "Why," Sabin would ask, "should Colorado, surrounded by Utah, Wyoming, Nebraska and Kansas—all with the lowest [tuberculosis] rates have such a [high] rate?" Her listeners left these sessions with pink leaflets explaining the issues at hand.

State legislators considered Sabin's activities a threat to the powerful and profitable milk and cattle industries. Many lawmakers spoke out against her and her bills. Governor Vivian expressed his skepticism, too. But Sabin pressed on.

Finally, her efforts were rewarded. In the statewide elections of 1946, every legislator who had spoken against the Sabin program was voted from office, including Governor Vivian. He was replaced by W. Lee Knous, who had actively supported Sabin's work. In fact, Knous thought Sabin was such a potent force that he called her the Atom Bomb.

A few months later, in early 1947, the Sabin bills were brought to a vote in the legislature. Four of out six bills passed.

For Sabin, it was a mixed victory. One of the bills that had been defeated was the one providing funding for a tuberculosis hospital—a measure that Sabin felt could wait. But she was keenly disappointed that the Cow Health Bill did not pass. The milk and cattle industries had managed to rally the legislators against it.

The defeat prompted Sabin to push harder. She held another dinner party

When W. Lee Knous defeated John Vivian in the 1946 election, Sabin and her supporters rejoiced because the new governor strongly favored passage of the Sabin bills.

at Brown's Palace, specifically inviting members of the dairy industry. By the dinner's end, she had convinced the milk producers that eradicating brucellosis would actually increase their dairy profits. She achieved a similarly successful result one week later, at a dinner to which she had invited meat producers. The next time the Cow Health Bill was brought up for vote in the legislature, it passed.

Meanwhile, the new governor of Colorado was starting to implement the other Sabin bills. The 76-year-old Sabin offered to help. Once again, she traveled around the state, checking on conditions, which often remained poor. "In one town," she reported, "women said they could see so much dirt in the milk that they did not use it at all."

But Sabin noted some encouraging improvements. At one stop, she said, "Our group saw a perfectly run dairy— run by a woman I am pleased to say— and a pasteurizing plant that is the last word in excellence."

In addition to troubleshooting for the governor, Sabin was appointed in 1947 to chair the Interim Board of Health and Hospitals in Denver. She tried to refuse the $4,000 yearly salary, saying, "I want no strings holding me back." But Denver's mayor insisted the salary be drawn. Sabin promptly donated it to medical research at the University of Colorado.

Part of Sabin's job as chair of the interim board was that she travel around Denver, trying to get people to submit to X rays. In 1949, after she had held the position for two years, the tubercular death rate in Denver had dropped by half. She remained at the post until 1951.

Sabin also wrote widely on the work she undertook. Her articles found their way into professional journals and other publications and were characterized by the same lucidity and clarity of prose that her biography of Mall displayed. "The People Win for Public Health in Colorado," published in the *American Journal of Public Health* in 1947, describes the fight for the passage of the Sabin bills. "The Ailments of the Health Departments," published a year later in the same journal, complains of the slow and tedious process required to bring about change. A paper on community organization was published in 1949 by the National Tuberculosis Association.

Throughout this period, Sabin continued to amass a number of honors, just as she had done in her younger years. In 1945, she received the Trudeau Medal, the most distinguished offering of the National Tuberculosis Association. Two years later, she was awarded the Jane Addams Medal for distinguished service by an American woman—an honor named after the American social worker who founded Hull House in Chicago in the late 1800s. In 1947, the University of Colorado also selected Sabin for its Medal of Achievement, and the American Women's Association granted her its Medal for Eminent Achievement. She accepted the presidency of the western branch of the American Public Health Association as well. In 1951, as Sabin approached her 80th birthday, she received another significant honor, the Lasker Award of the American Public Health Association, for outstanding achievement in the field of public health administration.

But all was not well in Sabin's private life. Her sister's health was failing to such a degree that the situation could no longer be ignored: At 82, Mary needed help getting in and out of bed. In addition, Mary's thinking had become confused and unpredictable. Friends gently suggested that she ought to live in a nursing home. Although Florence resisted the idea of institutionalizing her sister, the burden of Mary's care became a cumbersome one.

In the end, Sabin was forced to make a decision, and she made the only one with which she felt comfortable. She decided to care for her sister herself at home.

That December, in celebration of Sabin's 80th birthday, the University of Colorado dedicated its newest facility, the million-dollar Florence Rena Sabin Building for Research in Cellular Biology. The building contained the most modern equipment, and its construction was something that the always practical Sabin appreciated more than the awards she had won. When the ceremony ended, she went home to Mary, who had been too ill to attend the festivities. It was then that Sabin realized she would have to retire from public service if she was to continue to care for her sister. This time, her decision to retire came easily. After all, she had already accomplished what she had set out to do.

A short time later, in early 1952, Dr. Lawrence Kubie, a former student and laboratory associate of Sabin's, passed through Denver and stopped to see his old and esteemed friend. He found Sabin seated in an armchair before her television set, which was turned off. Piled on the table beside her, near a bowl of red roses, were volumes by Sigmund Freud and by Albert Einstein; her old friend Leo Stein's latest book, *Journey into Self*; J. Thomas Looney's *Shakespeare Identified* (Sabin was always interested in the theory that Shakespeare did not write the plays attributed to him); and a book by Homer Smith on the development of religion in human society.

Sabin greeted Kubie warmly and reportedly told him, "I've been thinking about human nature and about how hard it is to be a human being." She was going through a particularly difficult time in her life because she had just committed her sister to a private sanitarium. Sabin herself had been in and out of the hospital with pneumonia, and her physician felt that her illness had been brought on by the stress of caring for her sister. It was best for all concerned, Sabin was told, to have Mary nursed by professional help.

Even though Sabin's own health was deteriorating and she could no longer move about easily, she could not bear the thought of becoming inactive. Later in 1952, she gave a lecture (which was published as a paper the following year) on "Trends in Public Health," in which she compared the state of health in Colorado to that in California. Noting that California had taken an important lead in combating air pollution, she strongly suggested that Colorado heed California's example.

Also in 1952, the American Association of University Women established the Florence R. Sabin Fellowship to honor those who made important contributions in the field of public health. Like the building at the University of Colorado erected in her name, the fellowship was created to benefit others; for this reason, Sabin took great pleasure in the honor. Shortly afterward,

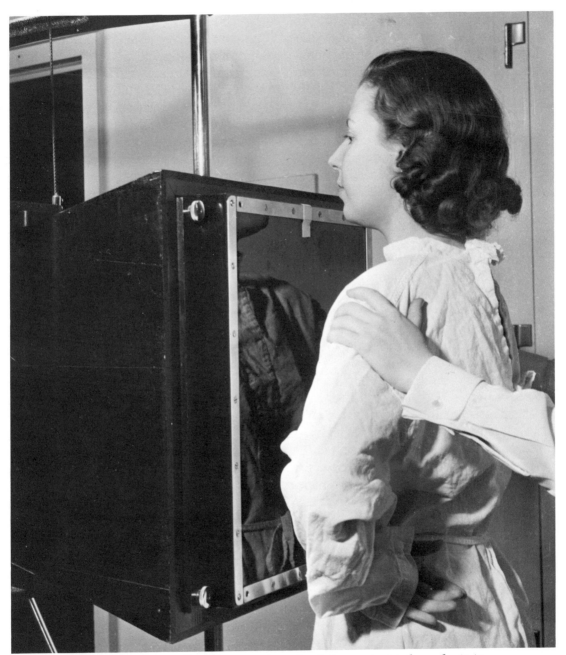

By 1949, Sabin no longer carried on the fight against tuberculosis in her laboratory; instead, she pushed for increased funding for early diagnosis. X rays were part of the public screening process she advocated.

Among the many tributes to Sabin is this painting, which is on display at the University of Colorado. The school's Florence R. Sabin Fellowship and Florence Rena Sabin Building for Research in Cellular Biology also honor her and make it possible for others to carry on the principal activity to which she dedicated her life: the search for knowledge.

she received the Elizabeth Blackwell Citation, which was named for the first woman in the United States to be granted a medical degree, and the Distinguished Service Award, bestowed by the University of Colorado.

Sabin was then interviewed for an article entitled "Are You Ready for the Scrap Pile Yet?" Among the other people examined in this essay were 82-year-old Bernard Baruch, an influential businessman and statesman who had advised former president Franklin Roosevelt; Roosevelt's predecessor, 78-year-old former president Herbert Hoover; and 92-year-old painter

Grandma Moses. Their interviews made it clear that none of these elderly persons was ready to stop working.

On October 3, 1953—the eve of her sister's 84th birthday—Sabin sat at home, happily watching the fourth game of the World Series, which was being played that year by the New York Yankees and the Brooklyn Dodgers. Having loved baseball all her life, she became an enthusiastic fan of the Brooklyn Dodgers when she moved to New York, and she enjoyed watching ball games on television. On this day, she watched the game with a private nurse: Sabin was recovering from yet another stay in the hospital.

As usual, Sabin cheered loudly for her favorite team. The Dodgers had lost two of the three previous games, and Sabin insisted to her nurse that the team needed her help; she had to cheer for them as much as she could. Just before Brooklyn came to bat in their half of the seventh inning, Sabin rose, with her nurse's help, for the traditional seventh-inning stretch. Yet it was to be her last moment of excitement. Sabin collapsed from a heart attack and died at the age of 81.

Sabin's will stipulated that her entire estate, which was worth several hundred thousand dollars, be given to the University of Colorado School of Medicine following Mary's death. Sabin's will also stated that the money should be used for both research and educational activities, her two lifelong loves. Bestowing such a generous gift was indeed a fitting final act for Florence Sabin, who had dedicated her life to medical research and always sought to help others.

After her death, Sabin's contributions to the pursuit of medical knowledge and her pioneering example for the thousands of women who followed her into medicine and research continued to be honored. In Denver, a new public school was named the Sabin School. A bronze bas-relief depicting her now hangs in the Denver General Hospital, and a statue of Sabin is one of two representing Colorado in the National Statuary Hall in Washington, D.C.

Many people have also chosen to honor Sabin by chronicling her brilliant career. No one has done it as succinctly, however, as the mayor of Denver, who published an article about her in the *Rocky Mountain News* immediately following her death. In expressing his city's grief at Sabin's passing, the mayor declared quite simply: "She was learned, she was wise, she was humble. She loved the world and every living creature in it."

CHRONOLOGICAL LIST OF PUBLICATIONS

Florence Sabin wrote the following journal articles and book chapters in addition to the books under her name in the Further Reading list. She also published book reviews and articles in German medical journals, as well as coauthoring nearly 50 more articles during her prolific career.

"On the Anatomical Relations of the Nuclei of Reception of the Cochlear and Vestibular Nerves." *Johns Hopkins Hospital Bulletin* 8 (1897): 253.

"A Model of the Medulla Oblongata, Pons and Midbrain of a Newborn Babe." In *Contributions to the Science of Medicine.* Baltimore: Johns Hopkins University Press, 1900.

"On the Origin of the Lymphatic System from the Veins and the Development of the Lymph Hearts and Thoracic Duct in the Pig." *American Journal of Anatomy* 1 (1901–2): 367.

"A Note concerning the Model of the Medulla, Pons and Midbrain of a New-born Babe as Reproduced by Herr F. Ziegler. *Anatomischer Anzeiger* 22 (1902): 281

"Tuberculous Pericarditis with Effusion; Repeated Tappings, Bacilli in the Exudate; Recovery." *Woman's Medical Journal* 12 (1902): 108.

"On the Development of the Superficial Lymphatics in the Skin of the Pig." *American Journal of Anatomy* 3 (1904): 183.

"On Flechsig's Investigations on the Brain." *Johns Hopkins Hospital Bulletin* 16 (1905): 355.

"The Development of the Lymphatic Nodes in the Pig and Their Relation to the Lymph Hearts." *American Journal of Anatomy* 4 (1905): 355.

"A Model of the Medullated Fiber Paths in the Thalamus of a Newborn Brain." *Anatomical Record* 1 (1906): 54.

"Further Evidence on the Origin of the Lymphatic Endothelium from the Endothelium of the Blood Vascular System. *Anatomical Record* 2 (1908): 46.

"The Lymphatic System in Human Embryos, with a Consideration of the Morphology of the System as a Whole." *American Journal of Anatomy* 9 (1909): 43.

"Description of a Model Showing the Tracts of Fibres Medullated in a New-born Baby's Brain." *American Journal of Anatomy* 11 (1910–11): 113.

"A Critical Study of the Evidence Presented in Several Recent Articles on the Development of the Lymphatic System." *Anatomical Record* 5 (1911): 417.

"The Development of the Lymphatic System," and "The Development of the Spleen." In *Manual of Human Embryology.* Vol. 2. Philadelphia: Lippincott, 1912.

"On the Origin of the Abdominal Lymphatics in Mammals from the Vena Cava and the Renal Veins." *Anatomical Record* 6 (1912): 335.

"The Origin and Development of the Lymphatic System." *Johns Hopkins Hospital Report* 5 (1913): 1.

"The Development of the Azygos Veins as Shown in Injected Pig Embryos." *Anatomical Record* 8 (1914): 82.

"On the Fate of the Posterior Cardinal Veins and Their Relation to the Development of the Vena Cava and Azygos in the Embryo Pig." *Contributions to Embryology of the Carnegie Institution of Washington* 3 (1915): 5.

"On the Origin of the Duct of Cuvier and the Cardinal Veins." *Anatomical Record* 9 (1915): 115.

"The Origin and Development of the Lymphatic System." *Johns Hopkins Hospital Report* 17 (1916): 347.

"Preliminary Note on the Differentiation of Angioblasts and the Method by Which They Produce Blood-Vessels, Blood-Plasma and Red Blood-Cells as Seen in the Living Chick." *Anatomical Record* 13 (1917): 199.

"Origin and Development of the Primitive Vessels of the Chick and of the Pig." *Contributions to Embryology of the Carnegie Institution of Washington* 6 (1917): 61.

"Franklin Paine Mall: A Review of His Scientific Achievement." *Science* 47 (1918): 254.

"Healing of End-to-End Intestinal Anastomoses with Especial Reference to the Regeneration of Blood-Vessels." *Johns Hopkins Hospital Bulletin* 31 (1920): 289.

"Studies on the Origin of Blood-Vessels and of Red Blood-Corpuscles as Seen in the Living Blastoderm of Chicks during the Second day of Incubation." *Contributions to Embryology of the Carnegie Institution of Washington* 9 (1920): 213.

"Studies on Blood. The Vitally Stainable Granules as a Specific Criterion for Erythroblasts and the Differentiation of the Three Strains of White Blood-Cells as Seen in the Living Chick's Yolk-Sac." *Johns Hopkins Hospital Bulletin* 32 (1921): 314.

"The Origin of Blood Cells." In *Addresses and Papers of the Dedication Ceremonies and Medical Conference, Peking Union Medical College, September 15–22, 1921.* Peking: Peking Union Medical College, 1921.

"Direct Growth of Veins by Sprouting." *Contributions to Embryology of the Carnegie Institution of Washington* 14 (1922): 1.

"On the Origin of the Cells of the Blood." *Physiological Review* 2 (1922): 38.

"The Extension of the Full-Time Plan of Teaching to Clinical Medicine." *Science* 56 (1922): 149.

"Studies of Living Human Blood-Cells." *Johns Hopkins Hospital Bulletin* 34 (1923): 277.

"The Opportunity of Anatomy." *Science* 61 (1925): 499.

"Research in Medical Schools." *Science* 65 (1927): 308.

"Bone Marrow." *Physiological Review* 8 (1928): 191.

"Chemical Agents: Supravital Stains." In *Handbook of Microscopical Technique.* New York: Paul B. Hoeber, 1929.

"Cellular Reactions in Tuberculosis." *Transactions of the Twenty-seventh Annual Meeting of the National Tuberculosis Association* 27 (1931): 195.

"Cellular Reactions to Fractions Isolated from Tubercle Bacilli." *Physiological Review* 12 (1932): 141.

"Bone Marrow." In *Special Cytology*, ed. by E. V. Cowdry. 2nd ed. New York: Paul B. Hoeber, 1932.

"Cellular Studies in Tuberculosis." *American Review of Tuberculosis* 25 (1932): 153.

"Discussion: Paper by Dr. C. H. Boissevain on Production of Tubercular Tissue and Hypersensitiveness to Tuberculin in Guinea Pigs." *Transactions of the Twenty-eighth Annual Meeting of the National Tuberculosis Association* 28 (1932): 161.

"Discussion: Paper by L. L. Daines and H. Austin on A Study of So-called Skin Lesions of Tuberculin-reacting Cattle." *Transactions of the Twenty-eighth Annual Meeting of the National Tuberculosis Association* 28 (1932): 181.

"Biographical Memoir of Franklin Paine Mall." *National Academy of Sciences, Biographical Memoirs* 16 (1934): 65.

"Women in Science." *Science* 83 (1936): 24.

"Development of the Cells of the Blood and Bone Marrow in the Rabbit." *Science* 83 (1936): 486.

"Chemical Agents: Supravital Stains." In *Handbook of Microscopical Technique*. 2nd ed. New York: Paul B. Hoeber, 1937.

"The Contributions of Charles Denison and Henry Sewall to Medicine." *Science* 86 (1937): 357.

"The Pathology of Tuberculosis." In *Tuberculosis and Leprosy: The Mycobacterial Diseases*, edited by F. R. Moulton. Vol. I. of the Symposium Series of Publications of the American Association for the Advancement of Science, 1938.

"Cellular Reactions to Tuberculo-Proteins Compared with the Reactions to Tuberculo-Lipids." *Journal of Experimental Medicine* 68 (1938): 837.

"Cellular Reactions to a Dye-Protein with a Concept of the Mechanism of Antibody Formation." *Journal of Experimental Medicine* 70 (1939): 67.

"A Theory of the Relation of the Reticulo-endothelial system to Antibody Formation." In *Blood, Heart, and Circulation*, edited by F. R. Moulton. Publication No. 13 of the Symposium Series of Publications of the American Association for the Advancement of Science, 1940.

"Cellular Reactions to Fractions from Tubercle Bacilli." *American Review of Tuberculosis* 44 (1941): 415.

"Biographical Memoir of Stephen Walter Ransom." *National Academy of Sciences, Biographical Memoirs* 23 (1945): 365.

"The People Win for Public Health in Colorado." *American Journal of Public Health* 37 (1947): 1311.

"The Ailments of Health Departments." *American Journal of Public Health* 38 (1948): 1508.

"Basic Community Organization: Cooperative Use of Leaders." *Transactions of the Forty-ninth Annual Meeting of the National Tuberculosis Association* 49 (1949): 315.

"Trends in Public Health." *American Journal of Public Health* 42 (1952): 1267.

FURTHER READING

Bluemel, Elinor. *Florence Sabin: Colorado Woman of the Century.* Boulder: University of Colorado Press, 1959.

Glazer, Penina Migdal, and Miriam Slater. *Unequal Colleagues: The Entrance of Women into the Professions 1890–1940.* New Brunswick, NJ: Rutgers University Press, 1987.

Haber, Louis L. *Women Pioneers of Science.* New York: Harcourt Brace Jovanovich, 1979.

McMaster, Philip D., and Michael Heidelberger. "Florence Rena Sabin." In *Biographical Memoirs, National Academy of Sciences,* Vol. 34. New York: Columbia University Press, 1960.

Phelan, Mary Day. *Probing the Unknown: The Story of Dr. Florence Sabin.* New York: Crowell, 1969.

Rossiter, Margaret W. *Women Scientists in America: Struggles and Strategies to 1940.* Baltimore: The Johns Hopkins University Press, 1982.

Sabin, Florence Rena. *An Atlas of the Medulla and Midbrain: A Laboratory Manual.* Baltimore: Friedenwald Company, 1901.

———. *Franklin Paine Mall: The Story of a Mind.* Baltimore: The Johns Hopkins University Press, 1934.

Yost, Edna. *Women of Modern Science.* Westport, CT: Greenwood Press, 1984.

CHRONOLOGY

Nov. 9, 1871	Born Florence Rena Sabin in Central City, Colorado
1878	Mother dies during childbirth
1880	Sabin moves with her sister, Mary, to their uncle Albert Sabin's home in Lake Forest, Illinois
1893	Graduates with honors from Smith College
1896	Enters Johns Hopkins University School of Medicine; father, George Sabin, dies
1900	Sabin graduates from medical school
1901	*An Atlas of the Medulla and Midbrain* is published; Sabin begins career as a researcher, working with Franklin Paine Mall
1903	Becomes assistant professor of anatomy at Johns Hopkins University; her series of papers on the lymphatic system is published
1917	Franklin Paine Mall dies; Sabin becomes chair of histology at Johns Hopkins; begins research on white blood cells
1924	Becomes first woman president of the American Society of Anatomists
1925	Becomes first woman elected to membership in the National Academy of Sciences; accepts position as researcher at the Rockefeller Institute for Medical Research in New York City; begins research on the pathology of tuberculosis
1926	Joins the research committee of the National Tuberculosis Association
1929	Receives $5,000 Achievement Award
1934	*Franklin Paine Mall: The Story of a Mind* is published
1936	Sabin begins term as a member of the board of the University in Exile
1938	Receives the $5,000 M. Carey Thomas Prize for excellence in scientific research
1939	Retires from Rockefeller Institute; joins advisory board of the John Simon Guggenheim Memorial Foundation; returns to Colorado
1944	Accepts a position on Colorado governor John Vivian's postwar planning commission as chair of the subcommittee on health
1945	Receives the Trudeau Medal from the National Tuberculosis Association
1951	Receives the Lasker Award of the American Public Health Association; the University of Colorado dedicates the Florence Rena Sabin Building for Research in Cellular Biology
Oct. 3, 1953	Florence Sabin dies of a heart attack

INDEX

PICTURE CREDITS

Janet Kronstadt was born in Washington, D.C., and lives in New York City. She holds a B.A. from the University of Maryland and master's degrees in Chinese as well as in creative writing from Columbia University. Formerly the editor of *Rehabilitation/World* magazine, an international journal on rehabilitation medicine, she has worked in book publishing for the past 10 years. In her spare time she is a competitive bicycle racer and triathlon participant. Ms. Kronstadt's short stories have appeared in *City* magazine and in an anthology of work first published in *Alternative* magazine. In 1985 she participated in the PEN New Writers' Series of readings held at the Endicott Bookstore in Manhattan.

Matina S. Horner is president emerita of Radcliffe College and associate professor of psychology and social relations at Harvard University. She is best known for her studies of women's motivation, achievement, and personality development. Dr. Horner serves on several national boards and advisory councils, including those of the National Science Foundation, Time Inc., and the Women's Research and Education Institute. She earned her B.A. from Bryn Mawr College and Ph.D. from the University of Michigan, and holds honorary degrees from many colleges and universities, including Mount Holyoke, Smith, Tufts, and the University of Pennsylvania.